THE RISE AND DECLINE
OF AN ALLIANCE

Cuba and African American Leaders in the 1960s

Ruth Reitan

Michigan State University Press
East Lansing

∞ The paper used in this publication meets the minimum requirements of
ANSI/NISO Z39.48–1992 (R 1997) (Permanence of Paper).

Michigan State University Press
East Lansing, Michigan 48823-5202

03 02 01 00 99   1 2 3 4 5

Library of Congress Cataloging-in-Publication Data

Reitan, Ruth
    the rise and decline of an alliance : Cuba and African–American leaders in the
    1960s
      p.   cm.
    Includes bibliographical references and index.
    ISBN 0-87013-498-1
      1. Afro–Americans—Relations with Cubans. 2. United States—Relations—
    Cuba. 3. Cuba—Relations—United States. 4. Afro–American leadership—
    History—20th century. 5. Afro–Americans—Politics and government. 6.
    Cuba—Politics and government.—1959. I. Title.
    E185.615.R45   1999
    324'.089'96073009046—dc21   98-39714
                                                                           CIP
Cover and text design by Michael J. Brooks

Visit Michigan State University Press on the World-Wide Web
    http://www.msu.edu/unit/msupress

THE RISE AND DECLINE
OF AN ALLIANCE

To

Eldridge, Assata, Kasi and Brock, for appearing when I needed them.

CONTENTS

PREFACE

Whenever I tell a colleague or a friend that for the past few years I have been researching the relationship between the Cuban government and key leaders of the U.S. Black Movement in the 1960s, the reaction is almost always the same: "*Was* there one?" This book represents an emphatic "Yes!" to this common response as it illuminates the shared history and ties between African Americans and the Cuban leadership throughout the 1960s. It was written in the hopes of first informing and then encouraging others who have an interest in this topic—scholars, students, or the curious lay reader of contemporary U.S. Black or Cuban history and politics or of the African experience in the Americas—to delve deeper into this rich and largely unexplored subject.

On a more personal level, this work was begun in an effort to explore for myself the ideas of legendary men and women, some of whom are still among us advocating radical change. These leaders were at once loved and hated, feared and idolized by many around the world. But who, really, were they? What did they stand for? How did they interact with one another as world politics changed throughout the volatile decade of the 1960s? Who betrayed whom? Who maintained alliances and held firm to their revolutionary ideals? Who faltered, and why? Who was blinded by his or her own racial prejudice? Who changed with the times? Who sought to hold onto power or status at all costs? These and other questions are grappled with in the pages that follow, and hopefully through the fruits of my journey, others can find nourishment for their own search as well.

This book also has contemporary political relevancy. As witnessed in Fidel Castro's 1995 visit to the United Nations in New York, he still enjoys the support and gratitude of a broad spectrum of African Americans, from radical nationalists to popular religious and cultural leaders. Yet these ties, at times, have been strained. In attempting to clearly define the nature of these relations and the major sources of contention between diverse U.S. Black leaders and the Castro regime in its first decade of rule, perhaps some of the misunderstanding, disappointments and anger can be avoided in the future.

Finally, this work seeks to provide food for thought to those who are still looking to the Cuban experiment for a possible way forward out of a racist and capitalist society. What must be kept in mind is that the race riots, radicalism, revolutionary hopes and violence of the 1960s are not just historical flukes, never to return with such fervor. As long as racism persists, as long as oppression continues, as long as cycles of poverty, violence and hatred are perpetuated, struggle will continue. This struggle will take various forms at different times in history, but there will always be those who, out of frustration, out of idealism, or for lack of a better alternative, will turn to revolutionary violence. As long as there is oppression, there will be revolutionaries to rail against it.

Although this work is based, in part, on interviews, whenever possible I attempted to consult other sources (documents, books, and articles in the scholarly as well as alternative press) in order to verify the interviewees' assertions and recollections. Where I have relied heavily on interviews are in those cases where no other documentation of the event is yet readily available, since the nature of the information provided was confidential and/or a personal assessment of events.

I wish to thank Drs. Jaime Suchlicki, Marvin P. Dawkins and the late Enrique Baloyra of the University of Miami for their insights and thoughtful suggestions for my work. I would also like to thank Dr. Tommie Sue Montgomery, Humberto León and our colleagues at the North-South Center for their support; Domingo Amuchastegui, for his valuable interview which helped to begin this process; Kwame Ture (formerly Stokely Carmichael), for never failing to respond promptly and enthusiastically to my letters—in spite of his life-threatening illness—and for putting me in contact with other activists; and Eldridge Cleaver, for his generosity, self-reflection and enthusiasm.

KEY EVENTS

Chronology of key events in the relations between the U.S. Black Movement and the Cuban government, decade of the 1960s:

February 1957   The Southern Christian Leadership Conference (SCLC) is formed, electing Dr. Martin Luther King, Jr. as its president.

September 1958   After monitoring the SCLC throughout its first year for Communist infiltration, the FBI opens a personal file on King.

1 January 1959   The insurrectional force led by Fidel Castro overthrows Cuban leader Fulgencio Batista.

7 January 1959   The U.S. government officially recognizes the Castro regime.

Summer 1960   National Association for the Advancement of Colored People (NAACP) activist and armed self-defense advocate Robert Williams visits Cuba with the Fair Play for Cuba Committee.

September 1960   A Cuban delegation visits the United Nations, staying at Harlem's Hotel Teresa; Castro meets with Malcolm X and other Black leaders; simultaneously at a rally of one million in Havana, Raúl Castro draws parallels among the struggle of U.S. Blacks, the Cubans before the revolution, and Africans in the Congo.

15–17 April 1960	The Student Non-violent Coordinating Committee (SNCC) is founded in Raleigh, North Carolina, to coordinate student protests.
June 1960	The Cuban regime expropriates American and British oil refineries after they refuse to process imported Soviet oil.
19 October 1960	The U.S. declares a trade embargo against Cuba.
Late 1960	The FBI monitors SNCC meetings.
3 January 1961	The U.S. and Cuba sever diplomatic relations.
15 April 1961	CIA pilots bomb Cuban airfields in preparation for the Bay of Pigs invasion.
17 April 1961	1,511 CIA-trained commandos invade the Bay of Pigs; almost all are captured and/or killed by the Cuban armed forces and populace within three days.
October 1961	Under pursuit by the FBI, Williams flees the U.S. for Cuba.
4 February 1962	Castro hails his regime as the genuine anti-imperialist vanguard of the Latin American revolution.
22–28 October 1962	The Cuban Missile Crisis takes place, where the U.S. denounces a Soviet attempt to secretly install nuclear missiles on the island; the Kremlin eventually capitulates and removes missiles.
1963	The FBI alleges that King belongs to 60 Communist fronts, which King vehemently denies; an FBI media disinformation campaign against him begins.
1963	Williams is appointed Chairman in exile of the Revolutionary Action Movement (RAM) based in the U.S.
1963	Herbert Muhammad, son of Nation of Islam founder Elijah Muhammad, visits Cuba.

1964	The U.S.-Vietnam conflict begins.
1964	Ernesto "Che" Guevara meets with a delegation of U.S. Black militants in Cuba.
8 March 1964	Malcolm X breaks with the Nation of Islam and establishes the Muslim Mosque, Inc., and the Organization of Afro-American Unity (OAAU).
April-May 1964	Malcolm X travels throughout the Middle East and Africa.
2 July 1964	The Civil Rights Act is signed into law.
December 1964	Guevara visits the UN; sends a letter of support to Malcolm X and the OAAU.
1965	U.S. forces invade the Dominican Republic; conflicts in Vietnam and the Congo escalate.
1965	Castro pledges support for the Vietcong.
1965	Talk of the impending U.S. Black-led revolution begins to appear in Cuban press.
21 February 1965	Malcolm X is assassinated.
April 1965	In a secret meeting Guevara voices his disapproval to Williams of the regime's approach to the U.S. Black Movement.
Early 1965	Guevara disappears from public view; soon resurfaces in the Congo to fight for decolonization.
6 August 1965	The Voting Rights Act is signed into law.
11–16 August 1965	The Watts Rebellion in Los Angeles takes place, resulting in 34 dead, 1,032 injured, and $40 million in property damage.
30 October 1965	Castro invites all persecuted U.S. Blacks to seek asylum in Cuba.
January 1966	The first Tricontinental Conference is held in Havana, establishing the Organization of Solidarity with the Peoples of Africa, Asia and Latin America (OSPAAAL).

May 1966	Carmichael becomes chairman of SNCC, moving the organization in a more radical direction.
16 May 1966	King agrees to serve as co-chair of Clergy and Laymen Concerned about Vietnam; he begins to make public statements against the war.
June 1966	Carmichael and Willie Richs of SNCC use the slogan "Black Power."
17 July 1966	Williams leaves Cuba for China after clashing with elements within the government and security forces.
28 August 1966	Williams writes his "Open letter to Fidel Castro" from China voicing his disapproval with members of the regime.
October 1966	The Black Panther Party for Self-Defense is founded in Oakland, California, by Huey P. Newton and Bobby Seale.
December 1966	Eldridge Cleaver is released from prison.
Spring 1967	Cleaver joins the Black Panther Party and is named Minister of Information.
Summer 1967	Race riots break out in 30 U.S. cities.
June 1967	Carmichael is inducted into the Black Panther Party as Field Marshal of the Eastern half of the U.S.
August 1967	The first Organization of Latin American Solidarity (OLAS) conference is held in Havana, at which Carmichael is an honored guest.
August 1967	OSPAAAL calls on revolutionaries worldwide to celebrate the International Day of Solidarity with the Black People of the U.S. in a militant way.
25 August 1967	The FBI, led by J. Edgar Hoover, officially launches a massive counter-intelligence program (COINTELPRO) to break the Black Movement and other radical organizations.
15 October 1967	Guevara is killed in Bolivia.

27 November 1967	King launches the Poor People's Campaign.
1967–68	Cuban representatives at the UN promise a military training facility near Havana to the Black Panther Party; a number of Panther delegations visit the site; Cubans train Panther members in weapons and explosives in Canada.
4 April 1968	King is assassinated in Memphis, Tennessee.
6 April 1968	Oakland, California, shootout between the Panthers and police; Cleaver is wounded and arrested.
June 1968	Angela Davis joins the Communist Party USA.
July 1968	The Panthers present documentation of the case against Huey Newton to the Cuban embassy in New York for their assistance; the day before, he was sentenced to 15 years for voluntary manslaughter; Newton's name begins to frequent the pages of Cuban press.
11 August 1968	OSPAAAL puts out a worldwide call to denounce the planned physical elimination of Newton.
September 1968	Malcolm X is hailed in Cuban press as the original bearer of enlightened leadership in the U.S. Black struggle.
November 1968	Cleaver goes into hiding and flees to Canada.
25 December 1968	Cleaver arrives in Havana in exile.
1969	U.S. government infiltration into the Black Movement becomes widespread.
January 1969	Carmichael leaves the U.S. for self-imposed exile in Conakry, Republic of Guinea.
May 1969	A frustrated Cleaver departs from Cuba for exile in Algeria.
September 1969	Cleaver establishes the Black Panther Party International office in Algiers.

INTRODUCTION

The 1960s witnessed the fracturing of a significant stage in the African American protest movement, namely, Civil Rights, and the emergence of another in its wake, Black Nationalism. On the international scene, the conflict in Vietnam and the cries for its cessation hit a fevered pitch; late in the decade, socialist-inspired guerrilla warfare was being waged around the globe and Cuba became a focal point of both conflict between geopolitical rivals—the United States and the Soviet Union—and admiration by those in struggle throughout the Third World.

During the first decade of the Cuban Revolution, close relations were forged between the new regime and the increasingly radicalized leaders of the U.S. Black Movement for a variety of reasons: the burgeoning militant wing of the Movement perceived a natural ally in the Cuban regime. A revolutionary Cuba under Fidel Castro offered solidarity and support to civil rights leaders and urban revolutionaries alike, publicized throughout the world the plight of oppressed African Americans and exemplified a successful eradication of "yanqui" imperialist control from their nation. Furthermore, Cubans fought against colonialism in Africa, promised to train U.S. militants in insurrectional tactics and weaponry and provided a haven for exiles. Perhaps most importantly to Movement leaders, the Castro regime claimed to have purged racism from Cuban society.

But tensions, misunderstandings and outright conflict shook the nascent alliance between these leaders. Consequently, while some of their relationships were long-lasting and mutually beneficial, others were ephemeral and ended in angry denunciations. Questions that this book seeks to examine include: What were the important elements and dynamics in these relations? What were the points of contention and convergence with regard to ideology and tactics? How were security concerns of both groups addressed within these relations? What expectations existed among the leaders? And finally, what led to the decline of Black Nationalism in the United States and the corresponding dissipation of Cuba's relations with the militant leaders?

In the discussion of the nature and significance of relations between the Cuban and U.S. Black leaders, new and alternative sources are intertwined with accounts that have been culled from individual leaders' writings and speeches over the past three decades. These sources are also weighed against relevant scholarly works, original documents, and newspaper accounts, and are placed in their proper historical context. The emerging view of these relationships is an attempt to address: (1) the key misunderstandings between the U.S. Black leaders and the Cuban regime; and (2) the stark absence of scholarly literature on this important topic.

Indeed, queries and discussions with activists and academics have revealed not a single book to date dealing with relations between U.S. Blacks and Cuba in general, much less among the leadership in particular. Carlos Moore's *Castro, the Blacks, and Africa*[1] does provide insight into a number of Black activists' exile experiences and general dealings with the Castro regime centering on the issue of the regime's racism against Blacks; however, these relations are not the main focus of Moore's work. Furthermore, the two most insightful personal accounts of an individual leader's ties with Cuba are Robert Carl Cohen's biography of Robert Williams entitled *Black Crusader*[2] and Eldridge Cleaver's *Soul on Fire.*[3]

Throughout this work it will be argued that a complex interplay of factors both drew these leaders together and at times drove them apart. The most critical factor in setting the parameters for these relations was the struggle within the Cuban leadership for ideological dominance and for the power to set security policy. Two conflicting camps emerged, centered around Ernesto "Che" Guevara's revolutionary vision and active promotion of armed insurrection on one end, and those who were part of the conservative, pro-Moscow leadership of the pre-revolutionary Cuban Communist party, called the Popular Socialist Party (PSP), on the other. The description of the latter camp as "conservative" should be understood in this context to mean a cautious or reserved approach, as compared to the Guevarist faction, with regard to the actions that it was willing to take in support of the U.S. Black militants; "conservative" also applies to the traditional Communists' views on security tactics and strategy in comparison to those of the Guevarists.

The island's escalating economic and military dependence on the Soviet Union severely crippled the ideological development and autonomy of the Cuban government in establishing foreign policy. This translated into an increasingly tepid view of the radicalizing U.S. Movement throughout the 1960s. Despite deviations in policy decisions and propaganda throughout the decade, a definite trend can be discerned toward an orthodox, Moscow-oriented ideology and national security position antithetical to the original views of Che Guevara and Fidel Castro. It will be argued that, while Guevara maintained his purist position and was thus forced from power by mid-decade, Castro, in order to maintain power, eventually either yielded to, or accepted the wisdom of, the Soviet ideology and security dictates. This polarization into factions—with Castro taking up the middle ground simply by passing through on his way to and from the extremes—made for erratic shifts in policy toward the U.S. Black leadership.

STRUCTURE OF ASSESSING THE RELATIONS

To arrive at the above conclusions, however, it is most meaningful to explore the relations as a whole within the following context. Relations between Cuban and U.S. Black leaders in the 1960s were complex and fluid, and developed under the restrictions and influence of certain variables. Due to the plurality of opinions inherent in each of these variables, tensions and conflicts necessarily arose. These variables include: (1) distinct political ideology and tactics; (2) issues of security; (3) convergent and divergent expectations; and (4) forces that contributed to both the decline of Cuba's attention to the radical elements within the U.S. Black Movement and the flourishing of ties with U.S. cultural leaders, Black scholars, and moderate politicians at the beginning of the 1970s.

Examination of these variables offers a more detailed view of the relationships, which then enables us to discover how and why certain alliances were forged and why at other times conflict developed. A clear understanding of the sources of conflict will help those who are seeking relations today to grasp their shared history and perhaps avoid the misunderstandings of the past. At the same time, a more comprehensive historical analysis of these relations may help to encourage further study of these significant variables.

First, regarding the Black leaders' *distinct political ideology and tactics,* it must be noted that a broad spectrum of Black Nationalist sentiment was on the rise in the U.S., to which the Cubans reacted in two ways. The pro-Moscow faction held firm to Marxist-Leninist doctrine and discounted nationalism in any form on the basis of its race-based analysis and thus segregationist tendencies. This group also denounced nationalism for its rejection of a strict focus on economic class. This faction, therefore, favored the ideology and tactics of U.S. civil rights leaders for their integrationist approach to struggle. The Guevarists, on the other hand, accustomed to challenging Moscow's orthodoxy, chose to focus on the revolutionary and anti-imperialist sentiment common to both the U.S. Movement and their own. They also agreed with the most radical nationalists on the promotion of revolutionary violence, a tactic that the pro-Moscow faction derided as "putschist" and divisive to the workers' struggle as a whole.

Individual racial bias or racism obviously plays an important role in the formation of one's political ideology. Authors Carlos Franqui and Carlos Moore charge that Castro's own racism clouded his ability to relate successfully to the Black revolutionaries; similarly, some U.S. leaders either harbored their own prejudices of Black racial superiority or were cynical after a history of betrayed alliances which prevented them from fully trusting the White Cuban revolutionaries.

But although ideological and tactical kinship was important, we will discover that in the volatile political environment of 1960s' Cuba, ideological convergence of U.S. Blacks with seemingly influential Cuban leaders in no way guaranteed positive relations with the regime as a whole. On the contrary, toward the late 1960s as the Guevarist philosophy was suppressed, Black exiles in Cuba were confronted with the *anti*-revolutionary reality of an increasingly bureaucratized state and gun-shy solidarity at odds with the official image propagated around the world.

Second, *national security concerns* placed limits on the solidarity and support that the Cubans were willing to provide, particularly as the traditional Communist Party faction gained dominance around mid-decade. Relations with the United States, or rather survival tactics in the face of a powerful and hostile neighbor, were the focus of these concerns throughout the decade. The issue of hijackings proved to be a dangerous political balancing act between Cuba's internal security and its sympathy for oppressed Blacks. Overt threats from the U.S. military, compounded by covert meddling and sabotage by the FBI and the CIA, added strain and an element of distrust to the relationship.

Intense debate within the regime centered around the best way to safeguard Cuba's national security. The Guevarists argued for actively supporting socialist revolution throughout the hemisphere while the traditional Communist party approach was to forge closer ties with the Soviet Union and thus cooperate with agreements made between the superpowers. At the root of this debate were fundamental differences in revolutionary ideals. It should be noted, nonetheless, that on occasion these two positions merged, as in the case of the collaboration of Cuba and the Soviet Union in a campaign of violence to overthrow the Venezuelan regime of Rómulo Betancourt in the first half of the 1960s.[4]

Third, although many expectations were met, divergent *expectations* among U.S. Black leaders caused bewilderment, disappointment, and anger, stemming most prominently from the realization that racism did in fact persist in Cuba despite official assurances to the contrary. Another failure in the minds of some of these leaders came from the promise that Cuba was truly a revolutionary society. The disenchanting combination of dwindling official support for insurrection, an emerging Sovietesque bureaucracy and the lack of personal freedom in Cuban society wreaked havoc on many leaders' faith in a socialist revolution as the desired political end toward which to struggle. As some leaders were frankly told by their Cuban hosts, the idea of supporting worldwide insurrection no matter what the risk died with Guevara's failed attempt to incite guerrilla warfare in Bolivia in 1967;[5] in reality, given the earlier ascension of the pro-Moscow faction, the idea was all but dead by 1965.

Finally, the reasons for *the decline of Cuba's attention to the radicals* were many. Most important in influencing relations with the Black Movement was the triumph of the traditional Communist Party faction over the Guevarists around mid-decade. A changing Cuban political strategy also contributed to the decline and was brought on, first, by the failure of the guerrilla "foco" theory advocated by Guevara, that called for cells of guerrilla fighters to be based in the countryside where they would engage in revolutionary insurrection and work among the masses; second, by Guevara's death in Bolivia and therefore an end of his influence on Cuban policy; and third, by an eventual turn toward Africa as Cuba's major international focus. The U.S. disengagement in Vietnam brought important changes as well. Within the U.S. Black Movement, evolving ideologies of the leaders themselves also played an important role, as did the fracturing of the U.S. militant organizations caused by both internal fighting and FBI repression.

Notes

1. Carlos Moore, *Castro, the Blacks, and Africa* (Los Angeles: University of California Center for Afro-American Studies, 1988).
2. Robert Carl Cohen, *Black Crusader: A Biography of Robert Franklin Williams* (Secaucus, N.J.: Lyle Stuart, Inc., 1972).
3. Eldridge Cleaver, *Soul on Fire* (Waco, Tex.: World Books, 1978).
4. Carlos Antonio Romero, *Las relaciones entre Venezuela y la URSS: Diplomacia o revolución* (The relations between Venezuela and the USSR: Diplomacy or revolution) (Caracas: Universidad Central de Venezuela Consejo de Desarrollo Científico y Humanístico, 1992), 42–43.
5. For nearly three decades, the exact details surrounding Guevara's death and the location of his burial site remained a mystery. The first break in the official silence came in November 1995. In the midst of an interview being conducted by author Jon Lee Anderson, retired Bolivian General Mario Vargas Salinas disclosed for the first time his involvement in the clandestine burial of Guevara and two dozen of his comrades in arms. Vargas asserted that Guevara and several other guerrilla soldiers were buried in a ditch near the airstrip outside of Vallegrande, a small town in Central Bolivia (Jon Lee Anderson, *Che Guevara: A Revolutionary Life* [New York: Grove Press, 1997], xiii).

    This pronouncement unleashed a flurry of activity. Under pressure from worldwide press, the Bolivian president ordered the military to locate and exhume the bodies of Che and his comrades. Meanwhile, Vargas Salinas was charged with betraying the army and was placed under house arrest [ibid., xv]. After several weeks of digging, the corpses of a few of the men were uncovered, but it was not until June 1997 that the remains of what was thought to be Che's body were exhumed. In mid-July, those remains were positively identified as Guevara's.

    A Cuban plane was dispatched immediately to Santa Cruz. In an elaborate display between Bolivian and Cuban officials, Guevara's remains were transferred to Cuban hands. In discussing this historic and healing event occurring between the two former warring nations, Bolivian minister Franklin Anaya cited humanitarian reasons for returning the remains of the guerrillas to their families and homeland. He also stated, "We hope this will bring to an end the historical period marked by the guerrilla movement led by Guevara." (*Star Tribune* [Minneapolis], 13 July 1997, 4).

    When Guevara's body finally arrived on Cuban soil, it was received in a grand ceremony near Havana. At the emotional event, Guevara's daughter offered her father's remains to the Cuban people. With a tearful and defiant shout of "Farewell, forever, until victory!" she repeated the words that her father uttered when he departed Cuba for Bolivia in 1966. A 21-gun salute sounded as the coffins of Guevara and three other insurgents were loaded onto military caissons, destined for their final resting point, a mausoleum in Santa Clara (*Star Tribune*, 14 July 1997, 4).

THE 1960S' U.S. BLACK MOVEMENT

Harold Cruse observed in *The Crisis of the Negro Intellectual: From its Origins to the Present*, "American Negro history is basically a history of the conflict between integrationist and nationalist forces in politics, economics, and culture, no matter what leaders are involved and what slogans are used."[1] This conflict can be traced back to the first great debates around the beginning of the twentieth century between the southern, pro-capitalist and accommodationist Booker T. Washington (1856–1915), and the Black nationalist, protest leader, equal rights advocate and northern intellectual W. E. B. Du Bois (1868–1963). By mid-century, the integrationist forces, led by Dr. Martin Luther King, Jr. through his struggle for civil rights and appeals to White liberals and Christians for support, once again dominated political thought and action.

FIRST STAGE: CIVIL RIGHTS (1950S–1965)

The racial integrationist approach to political agitation championed by Civil Rights leaders was supported by many in the nascent Cuban regime.[2] The latter agreed with the idea of integrated struggle to achieve an integrated society. Throughout the Civil Rights era, class distinctions were not dwelt upon in the mainstream U.S. Movement. Alliances were forged with any group—Black or White, rich or poor—who subscribed to the philosophy and tactics of nonviolent direct action. The issue of class would not become significant until the mid-1960s, when many forms of Black Nationalism would begin to reassert themselves.

9

The forerunners of the 1950s–1960s Civil Rights Movement included Washington at the turn of the century and Du Bois through his involvement with the Niagara Movement[3] and the National Association for the Advancement of Colored People (NAACP) in the first decade of the twentieth century. It is important to note, however, that Du Bois was a forerunner of virtually all factions of the unfolding Black Movement. Throughout his long life, he was "a socialist and Communist, an integrationist and advocate of a form of voluntary segregation, a black nationalist and a pioneering Pan-Africanist."[4]

Other important leaders who laid the foundation for the modern Civil Rights Movement were the anti-lynching protest leader Ida B. Wells-Barnett (1862–1931), the great civil rights lawyer Charles Hamilton Houston (1895–1950) and the political activist and union organizer A. Philip Randolph (1889–1979). The person and organization most responsible for the tactics and strategies used in the modern Civil Rights struggle were James Farmer and the interracial Congress of Racial Equality (CORE). This group, established in the early 1940s, was the first to promote such tactics as sit-ins, freedom rides and bus boycotts.

The most recent stage of the Civil Rights struggle is usually dated from the 1955–56 bus boycott in Montgomery, Alabama, and culminated in the passage of the Civil Rights Act of 1964 and the Voting Rights Act of 1965. The period's most famous leader, Martin Luther King Jr., was a Baptist minister who, through the Southern Christian Leadership Conference (SCLC), led mass protests of nonviolent, civil disobedience against racial segregation and discrimination. Indeed, King came to popularly symbolize the entire Civil Rights era.

The ideals of King and other Civil Rights leaders also influenced the creation of the Student Non-violent Coordinating Committee (SNCC). This organization was founded at a SCLC-sponsored conference at Shaw University in Raleigh, North Carolina in April 1960 in order to coordinate student protests. Within half a decade, however, SNCC's activities evolved from a regional focus on student sit-ins and registering southern Black voters to educating and mobilizing youth along more militant lines throughout the South and in city ghettoes around the country. Stokely Carmichael (Kwame Ture), SNCC's most powerful and riveting spokesperson, began to steer his faction toward a more radical stance, condoning revolutionary violence and self-imposed segregation. Many of these former followers of

King, upon his assassination in 1968, proclaimed the death of the nonviolent philosophy as well.

During the early part of the decade, which was dominated by integrationist, civil rights leadership, two forerunners of the soon-to-reemerge Black Nationalist stage were already actively propagating their alternative programs. The first was Robert Williams, the former NAACP leader turned advocate of armed self-defense and eventually socialist revolution. Within the NAACP, he was one of the most adamant challengers of the organization's position of promoting the philosophy of nonviolence. Williams was also the first prominent Black American to seek political asylum in revolutionary Cuba in 1961. In Williams, the most radical elements of the Cuban leadership were able to place their hopes of a vanguard force that could possibly begin the insurrection in "the belly of the beast," the United States of America.

Although the regime was officially in support of the nonviolent struggle for civil rights, the Cubans' revolutionary spirits merged with those of such men as Williams. The euphoria of revolutionary triumph gave the Cuban leadership the will to support Williams' violent tirades and calls for an armed uprising against the U.S. government over Cuban radio and in newsletters smuggled back to the United States.

But the man who was to raise the loudest voice against pacifism and integration in the early 1960s was the Black Muslim Malcolm X. Throughout his political career, Malcolm grew from cultural nationalist and staunch segregationist as a religious leader in Elijah Muhammad's Lost-Found Nation of Islam to Pan-Africanist envisioning a worldwide militant struggle of oppressed peoples everywhere. More than any other leader in that period, he paved the way for the reemergence of Black Nationalism in the late 1960s.

As nationalism and armed self-defense began to regain a large audience in mid-decade, the most ardent defenders of the pacifist Civil Rights struggle grew more publicly concerned with the economic issues facing the Black community, bringing the discussion of class back from the margins. This, however, was not enough to stem the tide toward a resurgence of nationalism in the face of mounting discrimination, violence, poverty and a worldwide convergence of common peoples' struggles.

Second Stage: Black Nationalism (1965–early 1970s)

The second stage, that of Black Nationalism, can be marked historically by the Watts Rebellion in Los Angeles in August 1965. This event was interpreted by many—including U.S. militants and the radical faction of the Cuban leadership—as a turning point in the Black protest struggle. U.S. Army and National Guardsmen were called in to put down the violent unrest that resulted in dragnet arrests of thousands, shootings of more than 800, and the deaths of between thirty and fifty African Americans.[5] Race riots continued to explode in the United States' urban centers and hit a fevered pitch in the summer of 1967. The Black Nationalist resurgence coincided with, and drew support from, the larger movement against the war in Vietnam. Its ideological antecedents were most notably Du Bois and the fiery leader of the Universal Negro Improvement Association (UNIA), Marcus Garvey (1887–1940), in the first half of the twentieth century, along with the proponent of Algerian decolonization Franz Fanon (1925–61).

While the resurgence of nationalism stemmed from the perceived political failures of the Civil Rights phase, it also grew out of one of its successes: a reawakening of Black pride. This celebration of Blackness manifested itself in many forms. Although loosely termed "Black Nationalism," this phrase is meant here to encompass diverse political strains such as cultural nationalism, Pan-Africanism, Black Power, and revolutionary nationalism. It must be noted that individual leaders and their organizations certainly bore, at various times, characteristics of different factions, and often times demonstrated a combination of some or all of them.

Cultural Nationalism

Thanks in part to the earlier promotion of this form of nationalism by Garvey and Du Bois, a significant number of African Americans in that period either adopted or already possessed to a certain degree a cultural nationalist perspective. In this vein, African Americans would wear African dress, take on African names, or observe traditional African holidays or religious practices. Cultural nationalists did not necessarily involve themselves in agitating for political power or for the decolonization of Africa, although certainly there was a blurred line between celebrating African culture and fighting for its survival or rebirth on the mother continent and in the diaspora.

In the increasingly politicized climate of the mid-1960s, however, those who did not participate politically were often ridiculed by more militant nationalist factions. Members of the Black Panther Party for Self-Defense, a revolutionary nationalist group who advocated a Black-led, socialist-inspired insurrection, used the label of "cultural nationalist" to deride others who they thought were not willing to partake in revolutionary violence. For example, Panther Party leader Huey P. Newton accused SNCC leader Stokely Carmichael of propagating an inferior type of nationalism, or in Newton's words, "pork chop nationalism." Newton charged that this reactionary form of nationalism bore an anti-socialist perspective, which had as its end goal the oppression of others.[6]

The Cubans had only a peripheral interest in cultural nationalists throughout most of the 1960s, since, at that time, the regime was not amenable to exposing the population to allegedly "foreign" movements of that nature. This brand of U.S. Black Nationalism, however, would gain favor with the Cuban regime in the 1970s, as ties with revolutionary nationalists decreased. Only then did relations with cultural nationalists flourish, as Blacks of this orientation visited the island to explore similarities between themselves and the Cubans who were, as they saw it, also fighting to preserve African culture throughout Africa as well as celebrate it within their own multiethnic society.

Pan-Africanism

The tradition of Pan-Africanism among U.S. Blacks can also be traced to Du Bois and Garvey, both of whom are considered founding fathers of this philosophy in the early decades of the 1900s. This type of nationalism is characterized by a concern for the culture and ancestry of African Americans and all Africans throughout the diaspora. These nationalists feel an indelible link with Africa as the motherland and therefore exhibit elements of cultural nationalism. Politically, Pan-Africanism calls for the uniting of all Africans to struggle for the decolonization of the African continent and to fight apartheid and discrimination against Blacks everywhere. Garvey's particular version of Pan-Africanism urged a uniting of Blacks around the world into one political organization. He also, for a time, advocated the emigration of U.S. Blacks back to Africa. In this way, Pan-Africanists take cultural nationalism into the realm of international politics.

A Pan-Africanist philosophy was again propagated in the 1960s, first by Malcolm X after his travels to the Middle East and Africa. Throughout the Black Nationalist phase of the last half of the 1960s, Malcolm's perspective had a significant impact on the ideologies of Stokely Carmichael and Black Panther Party activists. Carmichael would go on to become the chief proponent of Pan-Africanism adapted to the U.S. situation. The Black Panther Party acknowledged the philosophy's cultural value in stimulating self-respect and pride among the race, yet found its application outside of Africa to be misguided and confusing to the general population. The Cubans' strong positions against racial discrimination at home as well as apartheid, imperialism and colonization abroad won the interest and support of many Pan-Africanists, including Malcolm X and eventually Carmichael.

Black Power

Black Power has a variety of definitions, but according to Carmichael, the leader who first popularized the phrase in the 1960s, it had at least two. One definition was given in *Life* magazine as "'black people coming together to form a political force and either electing representatives or forcing their representatives to speak their needs,' rather than relying on established parties."[7] A second definition connoting revolutionary violence, however, was often explicated to more radical audiences: "When you talk of 'black power,' you talk of building a movement that will smash everything Western civilization has created."[8]

It is important to note that at the time Carmichael first called for Black Power, he had not yet fully embraced the tenets of Pan-Africanism. What these two distinct definitions suggest, then, is that the phrase meant different things in different periods of Carmichael's political development: Initially, Black Power signified a radicalizing of the Civil Rights struggle and a loss of confidence that the nonviolent philosophy could bring about adequate change. The second definition embodies Carmichael's embracing of Pan-Africanism. As he changed, so changed the definition of the phrase he popularized.

Author John White describes Black Power as a synthesis of the two definitions: "A militant black nationalism . . . with its connotations of racial assertiveness, separatism, and pride in the alleged African cultural and spiritual heritage of Afro-Americans," having its roots in Garveyism.[9] Panther leader Eldridge Cleaver concurs defining the phrase as a call for political power and a concern with the decolonization process in Africa.[10] In this way, it was internationalist in perspective, yet maintained the demands of the Civil Rights era for assurances of political rights for African Americans, but with a more militant, nationalist approach.

Cleaver saw those rallying around the cry of Black Power as largely Black college students who were interested in political agitation but who did not necessarily want to participate in political violence.[11] Most of what would be aptly termed "Black militants" would fall into this category, including the increasingly radicalized SNCC. Even some members of the political establishment, such as Black Democrats, would use the term "Black Power," when attempting to reach more militant African American voters.

The phrase, however, was picked up by many nationalist groups and was, in turn, used by the White mainstream media to invoke fear in White and Black moderates and conservatives. An adherence to Black Power would be given as proof that a leader or an entire organization was engaged in provocation and racism against Whites. It is not surprising, then, that Carmichael, as chief proponent of the controversial philosophy, was heralded by the Cubans as the caliber of leader who could guide the entire Civil Rights Movement on to a more radical course.[12] As he turned more and more toward Pan-Africanism, however, the Cubans and Carmichael's paths temporarily parted, and the regime instead embraced those leaders who maintained an analysis of struggle focusing on class rather than race.

Revolutionary Nationalism

Revolutionary nationalists were those leaders or organizations that were calling for a complete overthrow of the U.S. government and, usually, of the capitalist system. This would encompass those groups advocating either: (1) a guerrilla "foco" theory, adapted to the U.S. scene by Robert Williams; (2) an urban ghetto vanguard-led assault which leads by setting examples for action, promoted by the Black Panther Party and supported by such White radical groups as the Weather Underground, a revolutionary off-shoot of the leftist Students for a Democratic Society (SDS), or; (3) a mass-based proletarian struggle, political in nature but for the moment not advocating the use of revolutionary violence. Into this last camp fell Black communists such as Angela Davis.

These leaders had as their forerunners in the Black Movement such men as Du Bois in his later years and the socialist labor activist A. Philip Randolph. Although nationalist in many regards, this faction was not separatist: These leaders were willing to ally themselves with fighters of any race as long as they supported or were members of the peasantry, the proletariat or the lumpen proletariat classes and vowed to fight racism. They entered into alliances with the Cubans based on a convergence of class analyses; however, given their nationalist orientations, their class consciousness was infused with racial considerations. In an attempt to demonstrate a shared racial identity and minimize the ethnic distinctions between his regime and African Americans, Castro publicly drew attention to the mixed-racial nature of Cuban society. The regime promoted Cuba as an "overseas African country," and later, Castro described the population as a "Latin-African" people.[13]

Much has been debated over the position taken by the American Communist Party (CPUSA) toward the Black Movement: Was it genuinely "revolutionary," or rather racially ignorant and erroneously Eurocentric? The CPUSA rebuked both the urban vanguard and guerrilla fighting theories as putschist or opportunistic and deemed invalid the concept of Black Nationalism itself. Despite these disputes, all three of the methods—guerrilla "foco," urban ghetto vanguard, and mass political struggle—sought an eventual revolution of social classes and, usually, the overthrow of the capitalist economic structure. Most of the leaders in each of these factions desired the establishment of a socialist government eventually working toward some type of Communist system.

This study will argue that Cuba's foreign policies and relations with the U.S. Black Movement attempted to meet the challenges and opportunities posed by both of these distinct stages, Civil Rights and Black Nationalism. By mid-decade, however, as Soviet influence inundated the Cuban leadership, relations were more and more defined by reactions to the East-West conflict and the security concerns arising from it.

NOTES

1. Harold Cruse, *The Crisis of the Negro Intellectual: From its Origins to the Present* (New York: William Morrow and Company, Inc., 1967), quoted in John White, *Black Leadership in America* (New York: Longman Group, 1990), 1.

2. Domingo Amuchastegui, interview by author, tape recording, Miami, Fla., 23 March 1995. Amuchastegui was an official in the Cuban Ministries of Foreign Affairs and Intelligence and the head of the Department of Organization [vis-à-vis the Tricontinental organizations] during the 1960s and 1970s.

3. Formed in Niagara Falls, Canada, in 1905, this Du Bois-led organization agitated for full rights of citizenship for U.S. Blacks. It eventually was absorbed into the NAACP.

4. White, 51.

5. Cohen, 295.

6. Huey P. Newton, "Black Power and the Revolutionary Struggle," *Tricontinental Bulletin*, no. 32 (November 1968), 5; and quoted by Eldridge Cleaver, interview by author, tape recording, Miami, Fla., 20 January and 11 February 1996.

7. Quoted in *Life* (19 May 1967), 76–80.

8. Simon Glickman, "Stokely Carmichael," *Contemporary Black Biography* (Detroit: Gale Research, Inc. 1992), 49.

9. White, 13.

10. Cleaver, interview.

11. Ibid.

12. Amuchastegui, interview.

13. Fidel Castro, "Más tarde o más temprano, casi todos los pueblos tomarán las armas para su liberación" [Sooner or later, almost everyone will take up arms for their liberation], *Granma* (Havana), 16 January 1966, 3–5; "M. Fidel Castro souhaiterait que Cuba entre à l'O.A.U." [Mr. Fidel Castro hopes that Cuba enters the O.A.U.] *Le Monde* (Paris), 30–31 January 1966, 3; and Fidel Castro, *Angola girón africain* (Angola African Safehaven), (Havana: Editorial de Ciencias Sociales, 1976), 26.

THE INTERNATIONAL CONTEXT

F actoring heavily into the building of alliances between the Cuban
regime and the radicalizing Black Movement throughout the 1960s
were several international considerations: the deepening ties between
the Soviet Union and Cuba; trilateral dynamics among Cuba, the USSR,
and the United States; the role of China vis-à-vis the Soviet Union and
China's relations with the United States; the escalating war in Vietnam; a
growing internationalist perspective of popular struggle; the rise of guerrilla warfare in the hemisphere; and the role of insurrection in the decolonization processes in Africa and Asia.

SOVIET-CUBAN RELATIONS

The Soviet-Cuban alliance was in no way assured after the initial defeat of
Fulgencio Batista at the hands of the popular Cuban insurrection in 1959.
Fervently nationalistic, the new leadership led by Fidel Castro envisioned
a strong and independent country as well as a prominent Cuban presence
in the hemispheric struggle against imperialism. As the nascent leadership
slowly learned that ideology was not the only consideration in the
Kremlin's international maneuverings, a paramount goal quickly arose: the
maintenance of Cuban autonomy. This age-old battle for autonomy, first
fought against Spain and then the United States, was far from over in
1959, and indeed a new one was just beginning.

Relations between the Cubans and key leaders of the U.S. Black
Movement in the decade of the 1960s, then, must be viewed within this
context: On an ideological plane, an internal conflict was emerging within

the Cuban leadership over the desire to fight unjust regimes everywhere by supporting insurrection, versus the growing pressure to defer to the Soviet Union on matters of foreign policy. On a national security plane, a debate raged over how to achieve autonomy in the long run without jeopardizing Cuba's security and sovereignty in the present.

One camp, led by Ernesto "Che" Guevara, held that the way to safeguard Cuban socialism and independence was through actively supporting the overthrow of capitalist, neo-colonial governments in the Americas and replacing them with popular socialist leadership. Only in this way could Cuba's transition to socialism go unhindered. Che's view of national security was seamlessly integrated with his ideology of Communist solidarity, and therefore his policy decisions would always be made by choosing the most ideologically correct path.

The other camp was led by pre-insurrection Communists such as PSP chief theoretician and lawyer Carlos Rafael Rodríguez, Secretary General Blás Roca, Director of Information Aníbal Escalante, Fidel Castro's brother Raúl and the Minister of Interior under the Castro regime, Ramiro Valdés. These men advised that the safest route to ensuring Cuba's national security and, thus, its unencumbered march toward Communism, lay firmly within the Soviet camp. Therefore, developing relations with Moscow was to Cuba's ultimate strategic, economic and ideological benefit.

Although Castro supported a rapid move toward the Soviet camp prior to the 1962 Missile Crisis, he seemed to waiver somewhere between these two Cuban paradigms throughout the rest of the decade. The Missile Crisis severely affected bilateral relations because of the humiliation suffered when the Soviets removed their nuclear missiles without consulting Castro. As a consequence, decisions regarding the U.S. Black Movement were erratic as well.

TRILATERAL RELATIONS AMONG CUBA, THE USSR, AND THE UNITED STATES

In the first year of the revolutionary government, relations with the United States were uncertain. Washington recognized the new regime on 7 January 1959. Nevertheless, one of Castro's first measures the following day was to announce the permanent withdrawal of the U.S. military mission on the island. Castro had seemed motivated by a strong anti-American sentiment from his earliest days of political activity. This sentiment was perhaps initially expressed in April 1948 when he distributed anti-U.S. propaganda while attending an anti-imperialist conference in Bogotá as a student leader.[1] After coming to power in 1959, he confided to his closest advisors that the real revolution was now starting, against the United States.[2]

Relations had the prospect of improving that April when Castro was invited by the American Society of Newspaper Editors to visit the United States. While in Washington he met with Vice President Richard Nixon and Secretary of State Christian Herter.[3] Castro, regardless of what was said during those meetings, returned to the island determined to pursue his own agenda, launching the first agrarian reform law in Cuba the following month. This move sparked much concern among foreign capitalists. Their fears were compounded by Cuban émigrés' reports provided to the U.S. government that the leadership was fast becoming Communist.

In June 1960, American and British-owned companies operating on the island refused to refine oil imported from the Soviet Union. The Cuban government retaliated by expropriating those refineries.[4] However, the regime was burning its bridges with international financial interests faster than it could secure loans for industrialization. Since Cuba had withdrawn from the World Bank in 1960 and its sugar import quotas in the United States were being restricted by President Dwight D. Eisenhower, the regime was in dire need of alternative investment sources. Their desperation was answered by the Soviets' extension of their first low-interest loan later that year.

Throughout the summer of 1960, relations between the fledgling government and Washington worsened. The United States took its case to the Organization of American States (OAS), where it asked for hemispheric condemnation of Castro's government as a Communist threat. Castro, in rebuttal, acknowledged that the regime was indeed a friend of Communism but insisted that the United States was hypocritical to denounce him as oppressive, given its own discrimination against Blacks and Native Americans. From then on, the Cuban regime would express more adamantly its militant support for U.S. minorities.

In a sort of "push-pull effect," the Cubans moved toward the Soviet camp and away from their historical patron, the United States. That year Castro declared that his nation would accept Soviet weaponry to protect the island.[5] Soon after, Havana established relations with North Korea and the People's Republic of China. On 3 January 1961, the United States and Cuba severed diplomatic relations.

Castro first claimed Cuba to be a socialist state in April 1961 on the eve of the Bay of Pigs invasion. This affirmation was followed by his declaration in December of that year that he was, and would always be, a Marxist-Leninist. Still, the Soviet Union was hesitant to embrace the new government for many reasons, including Cuba's historical role of falling well within the United States' sphere of influence, the Soviets' concern over whether the Castro regime would survive and their hesitancy to support revolutionary leaders who came to power through violent means. The USSR stood a good chance of being drawn into a major conflict in defense of Cuba, a strategic risk the Soviets were averse to taking. Nevertheless, they finally recognized Cuba as a socialist state in April 1962.

Within six months, the Soviet's initial apprehension about a conflict with the United States became a reality. The October 1962 Missile Crisis arose out of a rapid, secret installment of Soviet nuclear missiles, bombers and military personnel on the island. The eleventh-hour decision by the Kremlin to remove the missiles was made without consulting Castro, thereby straining relations between the two countries.

Given this major international slight, the Soviets had to make up for abandoning Cuba lest they incur the scorn of the rest of the Third World and validate Chinese allegations of their betrayal of other socialist states. Therefore, for a brief time following the crisis, the Kremlin gave generous economic and military aid to Cuba and asked little in return.

Indeed, as long as other alliance options were available—notably China and the non-aligned nations—the Cuban regime still had significant independence in its decision-making, despite its increasing client role. It should be noted that this freedom has apparently been present throughout the regime's history. As Cuban scholar Theodore Draper observes, "Fidel Castro and his inner circle have never been innocent victims of circumstances; they have always been the engine of this revolution in perpetual motion."[6] Boris Goldenberg iterates this opinion by stating that Castro has always been the impetus behind major decisions and policies. Yet Castro, in his leadership, rarely had a clear, long-term plan of action, but rather used intuition and pragmatism to seize opportunities as they presented themselves.[7]

Carlos Moore agrees with these authors regarding Castro's active role at the helm of Cuban foreign policy. He maintains that, "Tensions between the USSR and Cuba would mount in direct proportion to the increase in Soviet aid. It was during this period, while the Soviet Union was doing its best to satisfy all of Castro's demands, that Havana was planning an ambitious militaristic foreign policy based on exporting the Revolution to Latin America and even Africa."[8]

Outside of efforts to make amends with Cuba after the Missile Crisis, the Kremlin's strategy toward the rest of the Western Hemisphere changed markedly. The Soviets and the United States were able to significantly increase discussions and agreements over a broad range of issues, including technological assistance and disarmament. Moscow also embarked on a path of military non-intervention in Latin America while instead seeking to develop economic and diplomatic trade relations.[9]

Secret talks took place, as well, between the United States and the Castro regime beginning almost immediately after relations were officially severed, and continuing throughout the decade.[10] These talks were hindered, however, by inconsistent policy, bad faith bargaining, and divergent perceptions on both sides. In the end they produced few, if any, positive results toward a lasting improvement in relations.

The very first meetings between high level officials took place at the Inter-American Economic Conference at Punta del Este, Uruguay, in August 1961, just six months after Washington officially broke off ties with the Castro regime. At the conference, Guevara met with a representative from the United States and asserted that Cuba desired a "modus vivendi" with Washington but would not negotiate the nature of the Revolution. President John F. Kennedy, who is said to have been "hysterical" about Castro, remained hostile to negotiating with the Cubans.[11]

Notwithstanding Kennedy's active pursuit of the overthrow of the young regime, others in the administration were more amenable to reaching rapprochement. Talks with the Cubans proceeded in 1963, yielding a proposed initiative by an intermediary which discussed normalizing relations. This initiative was on Kennedy's desk at the time of his assassination; his successor, Lyndon B. Johnson, put the proposal on indefinite hold, not wanting to appear soft on Cuba.[12]

Nonetheless, negotiations continued throughout Johnson's tenure, without the knowledge of the CIA, much less the American public. With the aid of U.S. journalist Lisa Howard and, later, Spanish intermediaries, at least three attempts were made between 1963 and 1968 by the Johnson administration toward rapprochement with the Cubans, under the preconditions that all Soviet personnel leave the island and that Castro cease subversive activities in Latin America. This policy of "positive containment" was reviewed by Secretary of State Henry Kissinger in 1969, and a more conciliatory scheme was then mapped out. According to Peter Kornbluh, no secretary of state before or since placed fewer restrictions on normalizing relations with the regime than Kissinger, with the result that the secret negotiations began, ever so slowly, to gain momentum at the close of the 1960s.[13]

Manuela Semidei's assertion that Castro offered to cease all subversive activity in Latin America as early as 1963–64 in exchange for improved relations with the Johnson administration seems less likely in light of the new perspective and evidence presented by Kornbluh et al.[14] Even if Castro had extended such an offer, it is doubtful whether he would have made good on his pledge. Throughout this period, Cuba was, in effect, actively involved in proxy wars with the United States through its support for Latin American insurrection. Then, in 1965, Castro pledged support for the Vietcong. Both of these facts illustrate Castro's siding with the Guevarist approach to Cuban security, which held that through Cuba's active participation, U.S. imperialism will find itself embroiled on so many fronts in open conflict that it would eventually be weakened or defeated, leading to its abandonment of foreign intervention, particularly in Cuba.

That same year, the Cubans saw an opportunity emerging in the United States to call international attention to the race riots and violence against Blacks, which was reaching a boiling point. Beginning at that time and continuing for the next five years, talk of racial war and the impending Black-led revolution was commonplace in Cuban media; it was here that the image was planted in the hearts and minds of Black militants that a racial paradise had been born in the Caribbean.[15]

Meanwhile, the East-West arms race was heating up as Nikita Khrushchev's statement in November 1964 suggested: "We will give the capitalist countries seven years at the maximum and after seven years we will be the number one power in the world."[16] At the same time, relations between Khrushchev and Castro solidified as a series of agreements on trade, technical assistance and defense were negotiated in 1963 and 1964. Consequently, Khrushchev's removal from power in October 1964 posed another setback for the Cubans. Their strategy of leverage that had proven effective with the Soviet leader would have to be re-thought, since tensions over divergent policies toward Latin America were mounting and continued to escalate over the next few years.[17]

These tensions were the result of a détente between the United States and the Soviet Union beginning in 1966. Moscow increasingly put pressure on the Cubans to cease their support of guerrilla movements in the Americas as negotiations improved with the United States over the next year. Nevertheless, at least officially, Castro held firm. In the years leading up to Guevara's death in 1967, Castro and the Cuban press denounced the pro-Moscow Communist parties of the Americas because they opposed the guerrilla "foco" theory and Cuba's involvement in insurrection in their countries.

Indeed, both Cuba's political autonomy and, some would say, its revolutionary soul rested on this policy of active intervention. As late as May 1966, Castro was publicly stating in a thinly veiled reference to the Soviet Union that Cuba refused to be anyone's satellite and instead firmly stood by its own independence.[18] That meant still holding to the principles for which Che was fighting in Bolivia. In the meantime, the Soviets reached another agreement with Washington that year.

Cuban-Soviet relations reached a nadir in early 1968, when oil shipments to Cuba were severely limited. This was most likely a move to bring Castro into line and make him cooperate with, among other requests, the cessation of his support for Latin American revolution. An emergency program of rationing which seriously touched all parts of the Cuban society and economy was implemented on the island. At the same time, a group of Communist Party members formerly of the PSP, referred to as the "micro-faction," were arrested and tried for alleged involvement in a Soviet-inspired plot to overthrow Castro.[19]

As revolutionary spirits and political options dwindled, Castro again salvaged relations with the Soviets in August 1968 and put his country irrevocably on the course toward satellite status. Immediately following the unpopular Soviet invasion of Czechoslovakia, Castro alone openly expressed his agreement with the USSR, stating that the measure halted a "dangerous evolution toward counter-revolution;"[20] two months later, the Cubans and Soviets were back on good terms after meetings in Moscow. With that endorsement, Castro appeared to have finally assumed the position as client of the Soviet Union and fell in line with the Kremlin's political viewpoints. Due to, first, a change of heart prompted by Guevara's humiliating defeat in Bolivia and, second, pressure from the Soviet Union, Castro ended his support for insurrection in Latin America.

THE CHINESE FACTOR

With regard to Cuban-U.S. Black relations throughout the 1960s, the role that China played was significant for a number of reasons. First, as long as the Soviet Union and China were at odds, the Cuban leadership had more leverage with the Soviets and therefore could maintain a certain degree of freedom in establishing foreign policy while at the same time winning concessions from the USSR.

By the early 1960s, the struggle between China—which became a Communist state in 1949 after a peasant revolt led by Mao Tse-tung—and the Soviet Union for hegemonic control of the socialist bloc had intensified. This conflict was not purely a struggle for military control and economic dominance, but also a battle for rank among the emerging socialist countries as the legitimate bearer of ideological leadership.

Historically, the conflict grew out of a number of broken promises and disappointments: the Chinese accused the Soviets of providing little assistance in the Sino-Korean conflict; of acting in an increasingly "imperialist" manner toward China throughout the 1950s; of seriously cutting back on oil shipments; and of reneging on an agreement to provide Beijing with nuclear weapons and instead calling back thousands of Soviet technicians.[21] China harshly criticized the Soviets' withdrawal of their missiles from Cuba in October 1962. Simultaneously, the Kremlin was attempting to expel China from the international Communist movement and place a wedge between Beijing and the Third World.[22] In 1969, tensions rose to a boiling point over a border skirmish along the Ussuri River.[23]

The Sino-Soviet split continued into the next decade; however, Castro, for various reasons, had already sided with the Soviets by the mid-1960s. But until that time, the Cuban leadership took advantage of the conflict, since it afforded many opportunities for Castro to play one power off the other and, therefore, to gain military and economic assistance from the Soviets as well as political space to maneuver independently in the Western Hemisphere.

Second, as U.S.-Chinese tensions eased at the very end of the decade, in a way similar to what had transpired after an improvement in U.S.-USSR relations, Beijing's support for insurrection withered. Until that point, relations with the United States had been at an all-time low, given the heightening of the conflict in Vietnam. The Chinese provided technical and military assistance to North Vietnam, and occasionally its territory was threatened or violated by the U.S. military.[24] Furthermore, Washington gave the impression to the Chinese that it was siding with the Soviets in the conflict between the socialist powers when it signed a bilateral, partial nuclear test ban treaty with Moscow in 1963. By the late 1960s,

China found itself sandwiched between two imperialists powers, sharing a border with the USSR and allying itself with the U.S.'s enemy in the Vietnam conflict. Fearing that an escalation in the Ussuri border dispute was more likely than a reinvigoration of fighting in Vietnam, China moved to create better ties with the United States for its own protection against the Soviet threat.[25] This led to an eventual improvement in relations with the Nixon administration in the early 1970s.

In line with this improvement, Beijing's support for insurrection in the Western Hemisphere diminished. It is important to note, however, that Cuba was never considered a vital concern to the Chinese, who were more interested in Africa and who, like the Soviets, had long considered Cuba to be within the United States' sphere of influence. At the beginning of the 1970s, then, it seemed that all parties involved—the Chinese, the Cubans, and the U.S. Black revolutionaries—had again yielded to Washington's dominance and ruled that insurrection in the Western Hemisphere was strategically and philosophically insupportable.

Third, on an ideological level, Mao was influential with both U.S. Black militants and the Guevarists in Cuba. The Chinese model and leadership were often cited by both groups to be correct in theory and practice. China fought its "people's war" against the United States in Korea in the 1950s and again in Vietnam in the 1960s. This active struggle against Western imperialism won the support of oppressed peoples the world over, including the Cubans and the U.S. Black militants.

In addition, the Chinese tactical position of the early 1960s was strongly supported by Guevara, Robert Williams and the Black Panther Party. All were advocating simultaneous revolutions throughout the Third World. Mao's *Little Red Book* was required reading for all Black Panthers. The Chinese leader won respect among many African Americans as the only head of state to forcefully condemn the racially motivated firebombing of an African American church in Birmingham, Alabama, in the summer of 1963. In his proclamation, Mao declared that discrimination against Blacks was part of a worldwide system of oppression and called on Whites in the United States to join the Black struggle against racism.[26]

Fourth, in the earlier part of the decade, as the dispute within Cuba over the ideological correctness of the two Communist powers was still undecided, it appears that a tentative compromise between the traditional Communist Party faction and the pro-Beijing Guevarists was reached. The official position was one of agreeing with the Soviets in the realm of international relations while siding with China in their embracing of popular struggle.[27] This precarious compromise, however, would not last long.

Although initially Castro proclaimed neutrality in this conflict, by early 1964, after signing two major agreements with Moscow, he began to show signs of allying with the Soviets, and, as a result, the Chinese began to see him as an opportunist. But a popular joke circulating in Havana at the time intimated that the Guevarist perspective toward the Chinese was anything but defeated among the Cuban people: "Our hearts may be in Peking [Beijing], but our stomachs are in Moscow."[28] Yet, around the time of Guevara's departure from Cuba for Africa in 1965, support for China's position was being suppressed, and it all but disappeared upon Che's death two years later.

Over the next few years, Castro again moved closer, both ideologically and strategically, to the Soviets. During the Tricontinental Conference held in Havana in January 1966, while Guevara was in the Congo, Castro tacitly lauded the Soviets' "concrete" support of Cuba over China's "verbal" solidarity.[29] Then, referring to the Chinese leadership as incompetent old men, he went on to call their regime "fascism flying under the banner of Marxism-Leninism."[30] Furthermore, Castro and the Cuban representatives included "peaceful coexistence" in the Tricontinental's final declaration, against the protests of the Chinese delegation.[31]

The Sino-Soviet split at that point widened to encompass a Sino-Cuban rift as well, which naturally drew Cuba closer once again to the Soviets. A public denunciation the following month of a Chinese conspiracy to subvert the Cuban armed forces further pushed the Chinese away from the Cuban leadership. At a 1969 world summit meeting of Communist parties following the Soviet invasion of Czechoslovakia, the Cuban delegation, led by PSP stalwart Carlos Rafael Rodríguez, firmly pledged their support for Soviet military action against the Chinese as well, a maneuver few other socialist countries supported.[32]

In response, Chinese propaganda in the United States became anti-Cuban as well as anti-White.[33] Subsequently, those Black militants within the United States who were still swayed by Mao's brand of socialism were calling into question their alliance with the Cuban regime. This wariness was compounded by Robert Williams' leaving Cuba for Beijing, where he sent back sweeping condemnations of the Cubans as increasingly conservative in their stance on U.S. Black liberation. Williams' experience was corroborated by Cleaver shortly after the latter departed from exile in Havana in late 1968. By mid-decade and beyond, the worsening of Cuban-Chinese relations paralleled the Cuban withdrawal of revolutionary support for U.S. Black Nationalists.

THE WAR IN VIETNAM

The escalation of the Vietnam conflict that began in 1964 posed a number of concerns and opportunities for the Cubans and U.S. Black leaders. The conflict was highly significant to Castro, Guevera, and others because they identified strongly with Vietnam, understanding that the ferocious U.S. attack against their ally could very well be leveled at the island as well.

Vietnam was unique in that, for the first time in Soviet history, the USSR did not stop the United States from waging war against another socialist state. The Cubans therefore feared that this would give the green light to Lyndon Johnson to attack Cuba without retaliation. Consequently, Havana viewed the mounting Anti-War Movement within the United States and around the world as a hopeful sign of salvation. Perhaps, through worldwide pressure, the United States would exhaust its imperialist tendencies and retreat within its own borders.

Increasingly throughout the 1960s, influential Black leaders of all political persuasions condemned the war as an atrocity against another people of color, and thus against their own brothers and sisters. Arguably, the beginning of the end of the Anti-War Movement and of the revolutionary period in contemporary U.S. politics in general came on 31 March 1968, when Johnson announced the cessation of troop build-up in Vietnam. However, since the war would not finally end until 1974, the international and domestic political landscape remained explosive over the course of those six years.

CHANGING WORLD VIEW

Another significant feature of the Black Movement throughout the 1960s was a reemergence of an internationalist perspective of struggle. Martin Luther King, Jr., who initially held a strictly domestic agenda, came to view the oppression of U.S. Blacks as inextricably related to the plight of the Vietnamese at the hands of U.S. soldiers. Similarly, Malcolm X began his political career as a disciple of Elijah Muhammad, calling for a domestic solution to U.S. Black problems, namely, a sovereign, Black territory within the United States. In the year before his death, however, Malcolm had turned toward a Pan-Africanist view of struggle while making efforts to do coalition work with non-Blacks in solidarity around such issues as the defense of international human rights.[34] Stokely Carmichael's own growth resembled changes in both leaders' perspectives as he evolved from taking an active role in the domestic Civil Rights struggle toward holding a Pan-Africanist view of world revolution.

This broadening view of struggle and solidarity foreshadowed the outlook of the Black Nationalist leadership which followed. After the 1965 Watts uprising, the most prominent militant leaders consistently embodied an internationalist view of struggle. Angela Davis within the CPUSA along with the leadership of the Black Panther Party worked actively to garner support for the Cuban Revolution as well as for revolutionary movements in Africa and Asia.

The Cuban government, for its part, praised the growing internationalism among the Black leaders. In the print media of *Granma*, *Tricontinental* and the *Tricontinental Bulletin*, the Cuban government and official press writers frequently linked the movements of the 1960s throughout the Third World with the U.S. Black struggle and pointed out ideological similarities between Ho Chi Minh, José Martí, Che Guevara and U.S. leaders.[35]

GUERRILLA WARFARE IN THE AMERICAS

The triumph of the Cuban insurrection set an indelible example for insurrectional forces throughout the hemisphere. The Cubans relished the role of revolutionary catalyst, and on 4 February 1962, Castro proclaimed his regime the genuine anti-imperialist vanguard of the Latin American revolution.[36] In his speech, Castro declared that South America was ripe for revolution, called upon the people to rise up, and pledged Cuba's unwavering support for their struggle. Until 1965, a significant number within the regime firmly believed in and propagated the Cuban insurrectional model as the correct way forward for all of the Third World.[37]

The year 1963 was a turbulent one for the nations of the Americas. Peru, Brazil, Venezuela, and Argentina were each experiencing political turmoil and a rise in insurrectional activities.[38] Throughout the decade, the Cubans took great interest in the guerrilla groups of Colombia, Venezuela, Guatemala, Peru, Nicaragua, and Brazil.[39] The Guevarist camp, which had gained momentum after the 1962 Missile Crisis, lobbied persuasively for their position that, since most Latin American countries refused to deal with a socialist Cuba, hemispheric revolution must be encouraged in order to reestablish relations.[40] That same year, Venezuelan and Colombian officials charged the Cubans with waging an undeclared war against their governments, given the high numbers of Cuban infiltrators into the local guerrilla forces; in Venezuela alone, a few hundred Cubans were reportedly aiding insurgents.[41] Cuba had also established military camps in the Sierra Maestra, the mountains where the Cuban insurrection first took hold, for Latin American revolutionaries to receive training and then return home to begin their struggle.[42]

As the traditional Communist Party faction again ascended to power around mid-decade after temporarily losing credibility in the Missile Crisis, debate grew over the ideological correctness and security ramifications of actively supporting revolution. Though it is difficult to know for certain, Moore maintains that even as late as 1967, Castro himself was still in agreement with the declining Guevarist camp regarding this issue. He states that Fidel "was convinced of the inevitable success of 'Operation Bolivia'," and was shocked to hear of Guevara's execution on 15 October 1967 by Bolivian soldiers.[43]

This is a surprising assertion on Moore's part in view of the unsubstantiated rumors that abound over Castro's complicity in the entrapment of Guevara.[44] It seems reasonable, however, that Fidel was still swayed by the Guevarist dream as late as 1967, if not its favorable political ramifications were more countries in the Americas to carry out a socialist revolution. What is clear is that by 1967 only a marginal few supported this strategy with regard to the U.S. Black Movement. Instead, by late in the decade, it was thought wise to support an insurrectional attempt only in those countries from which Cuba did not fear serious retaliation.

Guevara's capture and death shocked and demoralized the revolutionary movement worldwide. In Cuba, it also caused an abandonment of support for insurrection in the Americas. Within a year of his death, Cuba seemed firmly nestled within the Moscow camp. Telling signs of this were manifest in the conspicuous absence of any reference to guerrilla war in the hemisphere in Castro's January 1969 speech given on the tenth anniversary of the Revolution,[45] and in the cessation of programs on Radio Havana calling for armed struggle.[46] The weight of the disappointments in the United States, Bolivia, and other Latin American countries as well as pressure from the Soviet Union brought Castro to a position where, by the end of the decade, he seemed to many to be ideologically defeated, confused, and convinced that the Cuban model was clearly *not* the example for the Americas to follow. This demoralized attitude necessarily led to denunciations of Castro and the regime, such as that by Venezuelan guerrilla leader Douglas Bravo, who publicly accused Castro of abandoning him in favor of calculated alliances with the Soviet Union.[47] The crisis, for it was nothing less than that, also caused confusion and feelings of betrayal among some U.S. Black leaders.

GUERRILLA WARFARE AND DECOLONIZATION IN AFRICA AND ASIA

The internationalization of consciousness and struggle brought the U.S. Black Nationalists and Cuba together on African issues in the beginning of the 1960s. Between 1955 and 1961, twenty-one new states were formed out of former French and British colonial holdings in Africa. Many leaders of African countries, specifically those of Guinea, Ghana, Egypt, Sudan, Nigeria, Senegal, Mali, Upper Volta, Ethiopia, and Somalia, were sympathetic to the Cuban regime for at least two reasons. The first was that the Cuban model, as put forth in Castro's "Declaration of Havana" as well as in numerous speeches by Guevara, appeared to be directly applicable to an increasing number of struggles in Africa. As Moore states:

> Guerrilla wars were being fought . . . in the three Portuguese colonies (Angola, Guinea-Bissau, and Mozambique), while insurgents in the independent Congo were holding extensive territory. In the Camaroons, guerrillas of the openly Marxist Union des Populations de Cameroun (UPC) were actively reorganizing. Another Marxist group, the SAWABA of Niger, and the Senegalese Communist Party (. . . PAI) were also on the verge of launching guerrilla wars against independent states.[48]

These groups looked upon the Cuban experience with respect and as a guide to achieving the African nations' independence from colonialism and neo-colonialism.

A second reason for Africa's embracing of the Cuban Revolution is found in Cuba's militant foreign policy toward the continent. At the second Non-Aligned Summit held in October 1964 in Cairo, for example, Cuba pledged its unwavering support to bringing about and defending sovereign nations in Africa. Although its intentions have been questioned,

Cuba's Africa policy reveals an active participation in the decolonization process since the early 1960s. In 1963, Castro sent Cuban soldiers to fight alongside Algerians in the war against Morocco; soon after, Guevara left his government post as Minister of Industry to lead a column of Cuban and African insurgents in the Congo against the Leopoldville government. Cuban forces also defended the Guinean government and trained Africans to fight against the Portuguese colonial power.[49] Also in 1963, African trainees began arriving in Cuba from Zanzibar and Senegal.[50] As the decade progressed, it became evident that Cuba was far more willing and able to train a military cadre to fight half a world away than it was to support militants in its own backyard, the United States.

NOTES

1. Jaime Suchlicki, *University Students and Revolution in Cuba, 1920–1968* (Coral Gables, Fla.: University of Miami Press, 1969), 53–54; and Boris Goldenberg, *The Cuban Revolution and Latin America* (New York: Frederick A. Praeger, Inc., 1966), 149–50.
2. Carlos Franqui, *Diario de la revolución cubana* [Diary of the Cuban Revolution] (Paris: Ruedo Ibérico, 1976), 473.
3. Ricardo Rojo, *My Friend Che* (New York: Grove Press, 1968), 84.
4. Ibid., 87.
5. Lester A. Sobel, ed., *Cuba, the U.S. and Russia, 1960–1963* (New York: Facts on File, 1964), 120.
6. Theodore Draper, *Castro's Revolution: Myths and Realities* (New York: Praeger, 1962), 106.
7. Goldenberg, 183.
8. Moore, 146.
9. Ibid., 136.
10. Peter Kornbluh et al., "The U.S. and Cuba: The Secret History of Efforts to Normalize Relations," paper presented at the Latin American Studies Association (LASA) Conference, Washington, D.C., 29 September 1995; and Peter Kornbluh and James G. Blight, "Dialogue with Castro: A Hidden History," *The New York Review of Books* 41, no. 16 (6 October 1994): 1–4.
11. Ibid.
12. Ibid.
13. Ibid.
14. Manuela Semidei, *Les Etats-Unis et la révolution cubaine* [The United States and the Cuban Revolution] (Paris: Presses de la Foundation Nationale des Sciences Politiques, 1968), 161.

15. Baldomero Alvarez Ríos, ed., *Cuba: Revolución e imperialismo* [Cuba: Revolution and Imperialism] (Havana: Instituto del Libro, 1969), 432–37; and Fidel Castro, *Fidel Castro Speaks*, ed. Martin Kenner and James Petras (Harmondsworth: Penguin Books, 1972), 122–24.

16. "Dans sept ans, l'URSS sera la premiere puissance de monde" [After seven years, the USSR will be the number one power in the world], *Le Monde* (Paris), 9 November 1963, 6.

17. Stephen Clissold, *Soviet Relations with Latin America, 1918–1968* (New York: Oxford University Press, 1970), 3–65.

18. Castro, *Fidel Castro Speaks*, 205.

19. Comité Central del Partido Comunista de Cuba, *Informe del Comité Central del Partido Comunista de Cuba sobre las actividades de la microfacción* [Report by the Central Committee of the Cuban Communist Party about the Activities of the Micro-Faction] (Havana: Instituto del Libro, 1968).

20. Quoted in *Granma*, 24 August 1968, 2.

21. Michel Oksenberg and Robert B. Oxnam, *China and America Past and Future*, Headline Series, no. 235 (New York: The Foreign Policy Association, April 1977), 34; and Cohen, 257.

22. Moore, 145.

23. Oksenberg, 34.

24. Ibid., 33.

25. Ibid., 34–37.

26. Cohen, 251.

27. Rojo, 184.

28. Cohen, 266.

29. Rojo, 185.

30. Fidel Castro, *Le gouvernement chinois a trahi la bonne foi du peuple cubain* [The Chinese government has betrayed the good faith of the Cuban people], Pamphlet, 6 February 1966.

31. Rojo, 185.

32. Carlos Rafael Rodríguez, "Speech to the Conference of Communist and Workers Parties in Moscow," *Política Internacional* 7, no. 25 (1969).

33. Amuchastegui, interview.

34. Clayborne Carson, *Malcolm X: The FBI File* (New York: One World Books, 1995), 22.

35. See, for example, the *Tricontinental Bulletin* (Havana), September 1968, 1.

36. Castro, *Fidel Castro Speaks*, 146.

37. Fidel Castro, *Fidel Castro: Discours de la Révolution* [Fidel Castro: Discussion of the Revolution], ed. Christine Glucksmann (Paris: Union Générale d'Editions, Col., 18 October 1966), 239.

38. Rojo, 131.

39. Moore, 270.

40. Rojo, 133.

41. Moore, 179; and Ministerio de relaciones exteriores de Venezuela, *Seis años de agresión* [Six Years of Aggression] (Caracas, 1966).

42. Moore, 179.

43. Ibid., 270.

44. See Gary Prado Salmón, *Como Capturé al Che* [How I Captured Che] (Barcelona: Ediciones B., 1987); Steve Clark, "A Reply to Lies in the *New York Times* on Che and the Cuban Revolution," *Militant* (New York) 59, no. 47 (7 December 1995): ISR/5; and "The *New York Times*, Che Guevara, and the Cuban Revolution: a Further Exchange," *Militant* 59, no. 48 (14 December 1995): 7.

45. Fidel Castro, *Granma*, 5 January 1969, 1–6.

46. "Cuba Tones Down Overseas Radio," *New York Times*, 24 August 1969, 26.

47. Quoted in Moore, 277.

48. Ibid., 166.

49. Jorge Domínguez, Introduction to Moore, xv.

50. Moore, 179.

POLITICAL IDEOLOGY AND TACTICS

Since the triumph of the Revolution, an ideological battle had raged in Cuba that drastically affected the government's relations with the U.S. Black Movement, depending on who possessed the power to set policy at any given time. Although Castro seemed ultimately able to affect the nature of relations toward the militants throughout the decade, the faction or individuals who had his ear did not remain constant; furthermore, as bureaucracy flourished, many under him had considerable room to maneuver without Castro's discovering that a divergent agenda was being carried out. By mid-decade, the Guevarist faction was almost completely isolated from power, while Fidel—up until that time a tactical, and in many ways ideological, Guevarist—was increasingly insulated by the burgeoning traditional Communist Party faction from criticism and from a full understanding of the complexities of the hemispheric struggles. José Luis Llovio-Menéndez, Director of Capital Investments of the Sugar Ministry, Chief Advisor to the Minister of Finance, and Advisor to the Ministry of Culture in Cuba throughout the 1960s, described the nature and influence of the pro-Soviet faction, and in particular its two leading members, Ramiro Valdés and Raúl Castro, as "the most inflexible, coercive, and repressive strains within the Revolutionary Government."[1]

A brief history of the Communist Party in Cuba and the contentious relationship between many of its members and Castro is necessary here. The Cuban Communist Party was founded in 1925 and later changed its name to the Popular Socialist Party (PSP). On 8 March 1962, Castro integrated the two insurrectional factions (26th of July Movement and the Revolutionary Directorate) with the PSP, forming the transitional body of the Integrated Revolutionary Organizations (ORI). Within a year, a further step toward a permanent Communist party was taken when the ORI was dismantled and, in its place, another transitional organization, the United Party of the Cuban Socialist Revolution (PURSC), was established. On 5 October 1965, Castro officially established the Communist Party of Cuba.

It is important to note that the position taken by the PSP in 1953 toward Castro's 26th of July Movement and its attack on the Santiago and Bayamo barracks in the same year was anything but supportive. As PSP leader A. Díaz attested, "It is well established that our party took no part in the events in the East [Santiago and Bayamo], and in fact opposes these bourgeois-putschist tactics as incorrect, isolated from the masses, and obstructive of the mass struggle. . . ."[2] Even after Castro took power, distinct ideological and tactical differences separated him from the traditional Communist stalwarts. Boris Goldenberg states, "that even *after* the victory of the revolution the Communists were less radical than Castro whom they distrusted in spite of the pact which they had concluded with him in August 1959."[3]

From the Revolution's inception, Castro struggled to consolidate his own authority within the nascent regime, contain the traditional Communist Party faction's power and gain Soviet patronage. This was no easy task, as the "sectarian crisis" of 26 March 1962 clearly demonstrated. Soon after Castro had subsumed the various factions into the umbrella entity, the ORI, Aníbal Escalante, a PSP leader and Batista-era Marxist, began to dismiss other factions' leaders from government positions and replace them with his former party cronies. Castro waited until the right moment, when his popularity was at its height, to attack Escalante's "sectarian" attitude, purging dozens of PSP appointees from their posts and transferring Escalante to the *Pravda* newspaper in Moscow.[4]

Although some within the Communist Party did express their genuine solidarity with the U.S. militant movement, it was the experience of U.S. Black leaders in exile that by mid-decade this element had little influence within the Party. Those in solidarity with the militants expressed concern to Williams in the early 1960s that Fidel and the revolutionary faction were losing power to the traditional Communist Party stalwarts, who were then allowing the USSR to wield excessive influence in Cuban affairs and doctrine. Ongoing concern and debate proliferated over whether the Revolution, ideologically, was being betrayed.

As the decade progressed, more and more members of the PSP were appointed to positions of leadership. They occupied posts in the Agrarian Reform Institute (INRA), which oversaw the implementation and functioning of most rural programs; in the military; and at all levels of government.[5] The influence and ultimate triumph of the traditional Communist Party faction set the tone for relations between the Cuban government and the Black leaders in the nationalist stage which, most significantly, resulted in a decline throughout the 1960s of the regime's support for a U.S. Black-led insurrection, just as insurrectional forces within the United States flourished. This was due, as we shall see, to a marked shift in ideology and tactics within the leadership. The change from a radical stance toward the U.S. Movement to a largely conservative one had direct ramifications in the realm of state security.

At this point, it will be useful to contrast the distinct ideologies and tactics of the traditional Communist Party faction (also called the pro-Moscow or pro-Soviet faction, the PSP, or "Bourgeois Communists") with the Guevarist faction (also referred to as the "Revolutionary Communists") and to look at some divergent features of Castro's ideology. Although in many respects—most notably, tactical ones—Fidel concurred with the Guevarists, in other important areas—such as the issue of racism—there seems to be enough difference between them to warrant separate treatment in this chapter. The role of six influential Black leaders of the decade—Robert Williams, Martin Luther King, Jr., Malcolm X, Stokely Carmichael, Eldridge Cleaver, and Angela Davis—will also be detailed here.

All leaders and factions will be discussed within the following categories: (1) whether they were segregationist or integrationist; (2) whether they were nationalist, and if so, what type; (3) whether they displayed elements of racism, defined as advocating discrimination, believing that one race is superior to another, or holding other racially prejudiced views; (4) whether they held a race and/or class analysis; (5) whether they advocated violence.

Upon examination of the diverse Cuban and Black leadership in this way, we can see more clearly the reasons behind the convergence or conflicts that arose.

THE TRADITIONAL COMMUNIST PARTY FACTION WITHIN THE CUBAN REGIME

The pro-Moscow elements were solidly in support of the desegregation movement in the United States led by Dr. King. As Major Manuel "Red

Beard" Piñeiro Losada, head of the Cuban Directorate of Intelligence (DGI), explained to Williams, integration was the correct, progressive stance which would lead to a greater solidarity of the working class and eventually bring about an integrated, revolutionary struggle when the conditions were right.[6]

To the pro-Soviets, a colorblind struggle for integration was the only legitimate stance within the 1960s U.S. Movement. Their position was that they did not support Black Nationalism because of its divisive effect on the working class as a whole. They also feared that the "foreign ideology" of Black Nationalism, if disseminated throughout the island, would lead to secessionist movements in Oriente Province. Not insignificantly, Williams felt that the White Party leaders' concerns stemmed from a fear of losing their disproportionate representation in government to Blacks and people of mixed races;[7] in other words, to him, it was a selfish impulse based on racist principles masked in working-class, racially blind rhetoric.

Since the only organization in the United States deemed credible by the traditional Communist Party faction was the CPUSA, they disapproved of and even tried to sabotage Castro and Guevara's relations with most Black Nationalists. This Cuban faction, along with the CPUSA, derided the revolutionary nationalists as putschists, a conclusion drawn from the Communists' rigid interpretation of Marxist theory as applied to the U.S. situation. Black Nationalism, to them, seemed misguided at best and downright dangerous at worst.[8] However, this perspective also gave legitimacy to "Communist" racists who were already averse to seriously addressing the power differentials based on race within the Cuban regime and society. This strict interpretation of Marxism-Leninism gave those with racist tendencies an effective, paradigmatic shield with which to deflect nationalists' attacks on their authority.

The deep disdain for nationalists on the part of many Soviet, U.S. and Cuban Communist Party stalwarts was demonstrated by the manner in which U.S. Blacks were granted or denied entrance visas into Cuba. Unless a top official personally intervened—as was the case with Castro himself inviting Williams and Cleaver—the CPUSA routinely screened applications for Piñeiro's Ministry of Foreign Affairs (MINREX) visa department in order to bar most Black Nationalists from visiting the island.[9]

Given their absolute denial of race as a legitimate factor in one's identity within the class structure, these forces put total faith in the solidarity of the working class to eventually bring about a just revolution. The proletariat of the United States, which happened to be by and large White, could ostensibly be counted on to address the issue of racism once the workers had carried out a successful insurrection. In contrast to the Guevarists, the pro-Moscow Communists refused to engage in discussions with U.S. militants as to whether Marx or Lenin may have failed to anticipate contemporary problems in the Americas, acting as though these thinkers were sacred and their works could not be studied critically.

On the question of revolutionary tactics, the "Bourgeois Communists," to use Williams' term, were quickly retreating to their pre-revolutionary days, almost as if the Cuban insurrection had never—or should not have by Marxian scientific thinking—taken place. They shied away from actively promoting Cuban-style revolution or Che's guerrilla "foco" theory throughout the hemisphere, since this type of revolution was characterized as technically putschist and incorrect.

This faction, led by Escalante, believed that socialism could not be built by individuals nor could revolutionary stages be forced by a "foco."[10] They therefore disagreed with armed self-defense among Blacks in the United States because, first, it was said, the conditions were not right and, second, this violent tactic supposedly only divided the working class and gave the government cause to act in a heavy-handed, undemocratic manner toward all dissenters. But as many Black Nationalists saw it, the reactionary "Bourgeois Communists" used revolutionary slogans of Marxist working-class solidarity as a substitute for action.[11]

By 1965, the pro-Moscow faction had regained much of the ground lost in the sectarian crisis and the Missile Crisis of 1962. Moreover, observed insider Llovio-Menéndez, the old Party Communists continued to exercise indirect influence through their defender Raúl Castro.[12] Many Guevarists, including Che himself, were purged from key positions, and the nonviolent philosophy of King was again heralded in Cuban press and privately encouraged among the Black militants in exile.

THE GUEVARIST FACTION

The faction led by Ernesto "Che" Guevara supported the goals of integration and an end to discrimination and oppression of all people but did not agree with the pacifist tactics of King or his followers. Although he did not encourage nationalism at all, but rather an intense internationalism of oppressed people around the globe, Che did seem to grasp the complexities of both race and class. He therefore sought to understand the progressive nature of some nationalist factions, particularly revolutionary nationalism like that advocated by Williams and the Black Panthers. An anti-imperialist, he turned ever more away from all things European and instead embraced only those ideas and concepts that would liberate Latin America: "Mestizo, Indian, Negro or white."[13]

Che's opinions regarding race and class were not immutable throughout his life; rather, they kept changing as he sought new experiences and a deeper understanding of the world's people and its economic systems. Ricardo Rojo, a lifetime friend of Guevara's who first became his traveling companion throughout the Americas in the early 1950s, claimed that Che was "by no means a Marxist" in 1953; however, after seeking political asylum in the Argentine embassy in Guatemala after the fall of the socialist regime of Jacobo Arbenz in the summer of 1954, he had taken up increasingly radical politics. Guevara surveyed the political and economic situation of Latin America on his travels throughout the continent while in his mid-twenties. He studied the land reforms of Bolivia and Guatemala in the early 1950s and talked to peasants, miners, Indians, government officials, and radical dissidents from Chile to Mexico.[14]

Guevara concluded that the continental struggle was the offspring of historical, economic and political circumstances, the path of which could not be altered.[15] In a speech at the Afro-Asian Economic Seminar in Algiers in February 1965, which would come to be known as Che's economic testament, Guevara explained that the legacy of neocolonialism arose in South America, spread to Africa and Asia and was characterized by overt and brutal aggression, as seen in the Congo, as well as political penetration of the indigenous bourgeoisie.[16] The struggle for liberation against imperialism could not be divorced from the struggle against backwardness and would be brought about through both "political arms and firearms."[17] In Guevara's analysis, this quagmire of underdevelopment was manifested in the most abusive exploitation of the dependent countries and strictly resulted from the nature of the developed capitalist systems in their process of full expansion.[18]

Regarding the questions of class and race in the United States, in 1961 Guevara commented that the United States must be viewed as one evil block until the proletariat gains its consciousness as a class and U.S. Blacks organize a rebellion.[19] Che demonstrated his ability to adjust his class-based thinking to fit the racial situation of the United States in a meeting with Black militants in 1964. After defending the position that university courses in Black history were not necessary to a Cuban's education, he soon realized his error, contacted the University of Havana with instructions to prepare such courses, and told the U.S. militants that he understood that "it's a mistake to lump everything together under the heading of class conflict."[20] In response to his growing frustration with pro-Moscow forces' meddling in his relations with U.S. Black revolutionaries, Guevara decided that direct contact with the U.S. Movement was essential, and no longer relied on traditional channels of the CPUSA or Progressive Labor.[21]

Up until Che's death an important foreign policy instrument of the Cuban leadership with regard to the Third World was Guevara's guerrilla "foco" theory, publicized in Regis Debray's book *Revolution in the Revolution?*[22] Guevara, Castro, and other proponents of revolutionary violence propagated the idea that a new breed of fighter, the revolutionary guerrilla, could force the conditions necessary to bring about a violent overthrow of the existing capitalist structure. Guevara emphasized the need to develop a proletarian internationalist army bearing the noble cause of redeeming humanity by delivering, through force, the dictatorship of the proletariat.

At the close of the first Organization of Latin American Solidarity (OLAS) Conference in 1967, Castro iterated Guevara's opinion and called the notion that the vanguard must come from the national bourgeoisie a dogmatic absurdity in the Americas.[23] To Castro and Guevara, neither the economic class nor the race of the insurgents was an issue; they only had to engage in guerrilla fighting tactics, hold an internationalist perspective and have as their final goal a workers' and peasants' revolutionary government. Although revolutionary violence was an integral part of Guevara's ideology, it must be viewed as part of a whole complex development of revolutionary theory and practice with a goal of achieving a successful, guerrilla-led people's revolution.

The objective conditions for struggle exist, he determined, where unemployment and hunger are widespread and the working class is beginning to react to its situation. This reaction prompts a repressive response by the government and capitalists, which in turn creates more hatred against the oppressive forces. At that point, the support of an organized force is required, namely, the guerrilla "foco" that raises the possibility of victory through revolutionary violence.[24]

Guevara's explanations of the guerrilla "foco" theory were rooted in the assumption that the enemy would fight to maintain power, making a peaceful transition in the Americas impossible. A popular army, based in the countryside where terrain is familiar and favorable for guerrilla tactics, would be organized to counter the oppressors' army. He concluded that the leadership would be more secure in the country and therefore better able to command urban forces from that focal stronghold.[25]

Guevara maintained that a constant and firm attack should be launched on all fronts in order to eventually wear down the oppressors and bring about the total destruction of imperialism by eliminating its strongest foothold, the imperialist domination by the United States. This long, cruel war would lead to gradual liberation of and by peoples in their own countries and to the increasing isolation of the imperialists through international proletarian solidarity and swelling armies.[26] Castro, while affirming the belief that guerrilla warfare was the main solution for the oppression of Latin America, pointed out that Cuban revolutionaries would not be averse to any other expressions of armed struggle that might arise from garrisons or other sectors of society.[27]

The objectives of the Cuban revolutionary vanguard were to promote, "two, three, or many Vietnams." The goal of these many Vietnams, in Che's opinion, was the annihilation of the adversary in an armed struggle, and specifically the weakening of the United States, in order to obtain the strategic objective of power.[28] Castro reminded the world in his speech on the death of Guevara, however, that Che would not fundamentally be remembered for his military prowess. For Guevara, "warfare [was] a means and not an end."[29] The importance of the guerrilla struggle was to be found in the revolution itself which would culminate in the dictatorship of the proletariat. Developing true proletarian internationalism and internationalist armies that would serve the lofty cause of redeeming humanity was the ultimate goal of Che's tactics and ideas.

Throughout the decade of the 1960s, reciprocal affirmation that violent struggle was necessary to overthrow imperialism intensified among revolutionaries in the United States and Cuba. The Guevarists saw in the insurrectional rhetoric of Robert Williams, Malcolm X, the Black Panther Party and Stokely Carmichael a counterpart to Guevara's "foco" theory, albeit in varying forms and degrees. As late as 1970, a Cuban *Tricontinental Bulletin* editorial announced that any attempts to stop the ghetto revolts in the United States were futile since racism had been institutionalized and could only be purged through the radical transformation of the entire system, as the Black militant fighters had correctly pointed out.[30]

Despite public statements of support for revolutionary violence that lasted into the next decade, by 1965, the pro-Soviet faction had managed to block the actual support for this tactic considerably, particularly with regard to the U.S. Movement. At that time as well, Guevara was growing increasingly wary of the Soviets, their ideological influence within Cuba, and their less-than-revolutionary behavior worldwide. By the spring of 1965, as pressure to oust him and his philosophy from Cuba reached a fevered pitch, Guevara took the opportunity afforded by the Afro-Asian Solidarity Conference to instruct Cuba's patron state on how to be truly socialist. He told the audience that, along with economic assistance and fair trade, providing weapons and training to support revolution was the industrialized socialist nation's moral duty.[31]

Most likely as a consequence of this ill-disguised criticism of the Soviets as well as his ongoing ideological and tactical clashes with the Cuban pro-Soviets, Guevara went into hiding upon his return to Cuba. In a secret discussion with his friend Llovio-Menéndez in April 1965, he voiced his increasing discontent with the old-line Communist influence in Cuba: "The interests of Soviet ideology—and I mean Soviet, not Socialist—are promoted in Cuba by the same men who have done so much harm to the revolution. They are men without morality and without prestige and yet they become more and more powerful."[32]

That same year, Che all but admitted to Robert Williams, who had been in exile in Cuba for four years, his ideological and tactical defeat in the wake of his mounting isolation and divergence from the core of Cuban power. Guevara requested that Williams visit him to discuss the growing support in Cuban press and the Cuban Communist Party for the nonviolent philosophy of King's leadership. A recent *Hoy* article had praised that tactic and encouraged U.S. Blacks to act in this "correct" manner. Guevara expressed his and others' vehement disagreement with this advice to the U.S. Movement. Arrangements made between the two leaders for Guevara's expanded involvement with U.S. Blacks, however, would not come to fruition, as only days after their meeting, those closest to Che began to be demoted or transferred to the provinces, while Guevara himself was being removed from any ideological influence within the regime.[33]

FIDEL CASTRO

Fidel Castro's strong belief in the correctness of a unified struggle stemmed from the political turmoil of Fulgencio Batista's military coup in 1952. Castro claimed that after that event he vowed to forge a united front of all groups against Batista with himself as the leader.[34] Similarly, in the U.S. struggle, Castro fully supported the stage of Civil Rights because of its pro-alliance and integrationist stance.[35] However, as is argued in the discussion on tactics below, he firmly sided with the Guevarist faction on the issue of revolutionary violence and therefore disagreed with a completely non-violent tactical approach within the Movement as a whole.

Even as a youth, Castro strongly opposed racial discrimination and segregation. Throughout his campaign to seize power in Cuba, he actively advocated racial integration. Three months after the insurrection triumphed, the leadership abolished legal discrimination and segregation.[36] Unlike Guevara, Castro was Cuban by birth and has manifested a strong sense of territorial nationalism throughout his political career. Early on, his concerns were strongly anti-imperialist and nationalistic. He used Cuban nationalism successfully to sweep his regime into power. In the early days of the Revolution, Pérez notes, "Aroused too was a powerful surge of nationalism, one summoned by the revolution and soon indistinguishable from it."[37]

Part and parcel of Castro's brand of Cuban nationalism was a heightened sense of anti-imperialism, with the United States as primary culprit. In a letter from the Sierra Maestra, he wrote that he had realized his true destiny was the war he would launch in the future against the United States.[38] That conviction and his understanding of the merits of anti-imperialism and nationalism to rally support for insurrection enabled him to identify not only with the revolutionary nationalists within the U.S. Movement but also with a broad spectrum of nationalist and anti-imperialist elements.

Almost immediately Castro enjoyed overwhelming support from the Afro-Cuban population not solely because of his progressive and public stance against racial oppression and segregation, but also because the gains of the Revolution were initially felt most strongly among this segment of the population. Since Afro-Cubans were disproportionately represented in the masses of illiterate, unskilled and unemployed workers and peasants throughout the island, they benefited most from the immediate gains in wages, employment, land, credit, and education. Castro consequently won the allegiance of this historically marginalized group.[39]

But these early material benefits did not stamp out the legacy of racism, as much as the leadership would have liked to believe. The mere fact that Castro declared racism to be non-existent in Cuba just a few short years after the insurrection points to either a serious denial of reality or ignorance of an insidious historical fact. Jorge I. Domínguez, in his discussion on race in revolutionary Cuba, lends historical context to Castro's inaccurate assertion when he comments that "both white and black Cubans have always tended to deny that racism in Cuba even existed."[40]

Panther leader Eldridge Cleaver's experience on the island, where he spent five months in exile, reinforces this sociological observation. In his view, the nature of the regime's racism was and continues to be a lack of vigilance in addressing both unresolved, historical racial conflicts and the contemporary question of distribution of power.[41] He and others sensitive to the many manifestations of racism found that simple, government proclamations and progressive laws were not enough to erase this chronic societal ill.

Any discussion of racism in revolutionary Cuba must inevitably deal with the racism of Castro himself. Carlos Franqui, former head of propaganda for the 26th of July Movement, has given a fair portrayal of the Cuban leader, based on his more than two decades of close friendship with Castro. He states that Fidel's main limitation was his inability to empathize or grasp what it means to be Black, a woman, a worker, or anything other than exactly who he is, namely, "A first-generation Hispanic Cuban who grew up in an exclusively White, Catholic and Hispanic social and psycho-cultural environment." Franqui observes that Castro was not discriminatory but rather deeply paternalistic, because never in his life had he had to deal with the "other" as an equal. Blacks, women, peasants, and workers were all subordinate to him in light of his status in Cuba.[42] This, of course, only intensified after his seizing power.

At least three of the prominent U.S. Black leaders of the 1960s—Cleaver, Carmichael, and Davis—claim in retrospect that the regime was not consciously racially biased in its relations with the U.S. Black Movement or toward its Afro-Cuban citizenry. Each asserts today that the Cuban government was genuine in its desire to promote the liberation of Africans everywhere but was hampered from doing so by external pressures from the United States and the Soviet Union. Furthermore, all three maintain that, over all, the Cuban Revolution advanced the cause of freedom in Cuba for Blacks and Whites.[43] Unlike Cleaver and Carmichael, Davis never denounced the regime as racist and has consistently supported it.

Castro first proclaimed Cuba to be a socialist state on 16 April 1961. Six months later, he declared his lasting commitment to Marxism-Leninism. With this statement, Castro demonstrated his predilection for class analysis over race analysis. If one accepts Franqui's assessment of Castro's inability to discern distinct forms of oppression based on race or gender, then it seems plausible that Castro, more than Guevara, would have a tendency to side with the traditional Marxist-Leninist line on the issue of race. Nonetheless, given his strong nationalism, anti-imperialism, and leanings toward revolutionary violence, he would most likely have respect for, though be unable to completely understand the motivation behind, the U.S. Black Nationalist philosophies.

Goldenberg provides further insight into Castro's thinking when he observes: "But Marxist-Leninist and petty bourgeois 'putschist' ideas coexisted in Castro's mind, so that he was often to the 'left' of the official Communists, and was no less suspicious of them than they were of him."[44] This tends to confirm Castro's ability to entertain a nationalist perspective in addition to a class analysis.

Castro fully subscribed to the Guevarist methods of revolutionary violence for the Third World liberation struggle. But long before the triumph of the Revolution and his looking to Che for ideological and tactical guidance, Fidel was no stranger to violent struggle. He began his career in the hub of political agitation and "gangsterism" at the University of Havana in the late 1940s and pursued it in the early 1950s and in Bogotá in 1948. A year earlier he trained with other Cubans at Cayo Confites in eastern Cuba to wage an attack against the Dominican Republican dictator Rafael Leónidas Trujillo.[45] The daring, yet failed, attack on the Moncada barracks on 26 July 1953 proved Castro's ardor and transformed him into a national hero.

In his Second Declaration of Havana given at a mass rally of one million in 1962, he called for violent revolution throughout the hemisphere, since all options for a peaceful transition were deemed exhausted. In that speech he advocated Che's guerrilla "foco" theory.[46] In December 1966, despite the upsurge of pro-Soviet conservatism that was rampant in the regime, Fidel still openly declared his view that Guevara's "two, three, many Vietnams" approach was the correct one for Latin American and African revolution.[47]

Only months before Che's death, a headline in the 14 March 1967 *Granma* read, "Fidel: Those who are not revolutionary fighters cannot be called Communists."[48] Two months later, Castro, in the context of pressing Latin American Communist parties to support armed insurrection as the only path to peoples' victory, repeated, "Those who remain on the sidelines will cease to be Communists."[49]

After accusing the Venezuelan Communist Party leadership of treason, Fidel extolled the correct methods of the Black revolutionaries within the United States, saying, "They didn't talk about objective conditions before they seized weapons to defend their rights. They did not seek . . . a revolutionary philosophy . . . to justify inaction. . . . Here we have United States revolutionaries setting an example and giving *us* lessons."[50] Cleaver, Moore, and Rojo concur that Fidel maintained the ideological correctness of the guerrilla "foco" theory until it was finally put to rest with Guevara in Bolivia in October 1967.[51]

MARTIN LUTHER KING, JR.

Two years before the triumph of Castro's insurrection, Martin Luther King Jr. founded the Southern Christian Leadership Conference (SCLC), dedicated to the promotion of mass-based, nonviolent struggle for civil rights with the goal of U.S. racial integration. In time, King came to embody the Civil Rights struggle and the fight for integration around the world. He, more than any other U.S. leader, "inspired and sustained the struggle for freedom, nonviolence, and interracial brotherhood."[52]

King was in no way a Black Nationalist and rather disapproved of many of the more militant strains of nationalism that were again asserting themselves toward the end of the Civil Rights stage. King publicly criticized the phrase "Black Power" because of its connotations of violence and racial separatism. His comments alluded to the imminent split along racial, class and ideological lines that, by mid-decade, would fracture the modern Civil Rights Movement. Politically, he cast himself as a moderate between the apathetic masses and the belligerent Black Nationalists. Indeed, King seemed to use the menace of the extremes, such as the Nation of Islam, to win concessions from Whites to his moderate demands.

It is interesting to note that Malcolm X used this same political spectrum—with King in the middle and himself on the radical fringe—to lobby the U.S. power structure to grant King concessions. In early 1965, Malcolm X stated, "People in this part of the world would do well to listen to King and give him what he's asking for, because what he's asking for is right." He went on to warn that U.S. Blacks would win their demands one way or another, and if they were not won through King's nonviolent means, then other factions, like his own, would have to be more forceful in achieving what is rightfully owed to African Americans.[53]

Rather than nationalism, King exhibited an internationalist concern for the oppressed and poor. In 1959, he traveled to India where he made a spiritual vigil at the shrine of Ghandi, and also visited Ghana, Nigeria, and countries in Europe. In his acceptance speech upon receiving the Nobel Peace Prize in 1964, he linked up the U.S. Black struggle for civil rights with the larger issues of international human rights and world peace.

Unlike the nationalists, King reserved hope that racism could be overcome through Christian social responsibility, dignity and nonviolent political action. King maintained that the struggle to defeat racism could only be won by appealing to the goodness of people and always maintaining the moral high ground.

He showed no signs of a Marxist bias in his integrationist philosophy. A platform based solely on uplifting his own race, with the assistance of Whites and of all classes, was his early vision. As a student, King rejected Communism on the basis of its atheism, materialism and emphasis on class antagonisms, although he found common ground with its general concern for society and the oppressed.[54]

Although FBI Director J. Edgar Hoover and other right-wing extremists went to great lengths to demonstrate that the "red hand" of the CPUSA and Castro were behind King's leadership and the Civil Rights Movement in general, these allegations were erroneous and could be easily disproved by an objective investigation. Yet the accusations damaged King's credibility. He vehemently denied rumors of Communist infiltration into the SCLC and allegations that he was a member of "sixty Communist fronts," an outrageous charge made by paid FBI informant Karl Prussian in 1963.[55] In a 1964 statement, King blasted Hoover for fueling these falsehoods about him and his organization. He went on to call Communism "crippling totalitarianism" and assured that the SCLC did not take advice from, nor did it accept as members, people with "Communist leanings."[56]

King chose to enter into alliances with people regardless of race or class. He felt that strength lay in bringing the White majority into the Black struggle for equal rights. To this end, he appealed to the White liberal's conscience. As for the issue of class, the history of the 382-day Montgomery, Alabama bus boycott taught King and others that mass protest in the Black community could most effectively be organized through the Black churches, in good part because of their integration of social classes and political ideologies.[57]

As the struggle wore on, however, King demonstrated an emerging class consciousness. He moved first from agitating primarily for racial integration to a focus on political and economic rights; he then broadened his philosophy and saw a need to work for a coalition of poor Blacks and Whites in the U.S.; and finally, he became more and more critical of the United States' involvement in Vietnam and of the U.S. capitalist system.[58] Each of these stands displays his evolving class-based, internationalist and anti-imperialist perspective.

The issues of poverty and U.S. imperialism were to King intimately connected and were the focal point of the last years of his life.[59] His realization of this connection and his subsequent call to action were brought on by an escalation of urban riots and the war in Vietnam. King's new focus supported the claim that he was becoming more radical in his final years. While in Chicago in 1966 to challenge school segregation, poor housing, unemployment and job discrimination, he was challenged on both personal and ideological grounds. At that time he became increasingly drawn to the democratic socialism of such countries as Sweden and began making louder demands for drastic redistribution of wealth and political power.[60] The following year, he attempted to organize an interracial coalition of poor people along class, rather than racial, lines. The Poor People's Campaign was launched in Washington D.C. to push Congress to enact legislation that would massively fund an anti-poverty program, but the march which King had envisioned would not take place until after his death.

In the last major speech before his assassination, King called for a recognition of W. E. B. Du Bois as an empathetic and brilliant African American leader, as a defender of the oppressed, and as a Communist. To deny his Communist ideology, King asserted, was to play into the hands of McCarthyites who sought to divide the Black community and debilitate the Black Movement. This open acknowledgment of Du Bois's Communism in a tribute on the centennial of his birth pointed to King's willingness to entertain more radical ideologies toward the end of his life. It also highlighted his growing defiance of the harassment by the FBI for alleged Communist infiltration of the SCLC as well as his unwillingness to allow red-baiters to dictate coalitions among progressive Whites and Blacks.

There would appear to be little doubt that King was indeed going in a more radical direction, but one can only speculate as to what sort of identification he would have had with the Cuban struggle in the future. It is plausible that he was moving toward supporting the Cuban Revolution, but his life was snuffed out before he felt it politically responsible to do so.

King's immediate forerunner of nonviolent political action was the Black socialist A. Philip Randolph, who planned acts of civil disobedience in the 1940s based on the Ghandian example of peacefully forcing concessions from government. Another early proponent in the Black community of Ghandi's techniques and philosophies was James Farmer, who practiced the Indian's teachings through the Congress of Racial Equality (CORE), which he helped found in 1942.

Labeling it a second-class method, King concluded that the armed self-defense tactic advocated by Robert Williams and Malcolm X in the early 1960s was immoral and incorrect for the Movement. His own pacifist tactics and ideology stemmed from a spiritual grounding in Christian convictions, enhanced by the teachings of Mohandas Ghandi. He and the SCLC put into practice the tactics of direct nonviolent action. As he held firmly to his convictions, the divergent tactical stances of King and the more militant strains of the Black Movement were not resolved before his death.

Although, as mentioned previously, the Guevarist faction disagreed with the nonviolent approach to struggle, the pro-Soviet elements favored King's coalition-building philosophies and thought that his tactics were well-suited for that stage of the struggle.[61] Despite widespread rumors to the contrary and exhaustive investigations by the U.S. government, evidently no contact on either side was made to initiate a relationship between the Cubans and the Civil Rights leader. The Cubans, nonetheless, sent King messages of solidarity through the media. The traditional Communist Party faction viewed King as the most capable leader for bringing the Black militants into the larger, Anti-War Movement, and mourned his death in 1968.[62]

King was one of the first U.S. leaders of international status to come out against the war in Vietnam, serving as co-chair of Clergy and Laymen Concerned about Vietnam. In a speech given in early 1967, the year before his assassination, he expressed sympathy for the horrors suffered by the Vietnamese and voiced solidarity with the Vietcong and the revolutionary movements of the Third World. In May, he spoke of Ho Chi Minh as a popular and dedicated leader of a movement fighting against a corrupt dictator. Toward the end of his life, King became more and more convinced of the intimate connection between poverty, racism, U.S. imperialism and his own country's militarism.[63] Although it is doubtful that King would have ever abandoned his principle of nonviolence, he seemed to have a growing understanding of, even tolerance for, the desire for violent struggle at home and around the world. As a sad paradox to King's life, in the week following his assassination in Memphis on 4 April 1968, riots erupted in 125 cities across the United States.

ROBERT WILLIAMS

Robert Williams began his political career like most southern African Americans in the 1950s: as a supporter of racial integration. He joined the NAACP in 1955 in his hometown of Monroe, North Carolina, but he soon became embroiled in ongoing disputes with national leadership over the appropriateness of armed self-defense and his outspoken views on Cuba, after traveling to the island in the spring of 1960 and returning a proponent of the young revolution. Still, he was an ardent supporter of both integration and armed self-defense until he fled the United States for Cuba in 1961. While in exile, however, his views on integration changed radically: In 1968, he accepted the appointment of the first chief of state of the Republic of New Africa, a separatist organization that was seeking from the U.S. government the transfer of five southern states in which to begin a sovereign Black country.[64]

While initially only advocating armed self-defense for Blacks' protection in the fight for integration into U.S. society, Williams was eventually led by his experiences to embrace revolutionary nationalism. This made him an immediate forerunner of groups such as the Black Panther Party, who advocated the forceful overthrow of the U.S. government. Within his first year of exile in Havana, he showed signs of this transformation from militant integrationist fighter to revolutionary nationalist. He perceived that the entire system had to change for Blacks to regain their nationhood and concluded that U.S. Blacks, Africans, Asians and Cubans all had a common enemy: "Savage white imperialists."

In 1963, Williams was appointed Chairman in exile of the Revolutionary Action Movement (RAM) based in the United States, whose primary function was to establish and maintain contact with the most militant members of SNCC, the Nation of Islam, CORE and the NAACP. The impetus was to create a theoretical platform from which to launch the "Black Liberation Movement."[65] Although willing to work with a broad range of nationalists, Williams did react negatively to strict cultural nationalists. Those who took on superficial African trappings were doing so, he thought, in an attempt to escape their duty to work for equality and justice.[66]

Despite his lifelong experience with discrimination and institutionalized racism in the United States, Williams maintained that it was an error to reject the help of well-intentioned Whites. He accepted assistance from Whites throughout his political career and recognized that, "[our struggle] must not be anti-white, but anti-oppression and injustice. Uncle Toms should be as much a target as racist whites."[67] However, he was displeased with the lack of dedication and discipline he saw among many Whites in the "New Left" who visited Cuba, and consequently began to advocate minority-led revolution in 1963.[68]

Although he did not initially consider himself a Marxist, Williams did possess a class perspective in regard to the Black elite who sought to deny a rising racial consciousness and hold the Black masses in subjugation. He also endorsed the Cuban and Chinese revolutions as correct in view of the distinct historical development and ethnic makeup of those countries.

Despite his class consciousness, Williams became averse to pro-Soviet Communists. His conflicts with the Communist parties worldwide began in the United States before his exile. Initially impressed by the CPUSA in the early 1940s—given their platform of equal rights, their visibly Black leadership, and their legal defense of Blacks[69]—he became disillusioned with the discrimination he continued to see within unions and doubted that White workers in the United States would ever overcome their racism with regard to the Black proletariat.

He refused to join the CPUSA because of his deeply held belief that he could not join an organization that did not hold as its primary concern Black liberation and did not have a majority Black membership. This rift with the CPUSA carried over while he was in exile to the traditional Communist Party faction, or "Bourgeois Communists," as he perjoratively called them. Among the latter, he encountered the same unchallenged faith in the White proletarian majority. These leaders instructed Williams that the revolution must be a joint effort, since the vast majority of workers in the United States were White, and that a separate, Black revolt was counterproductive. Williams, however, felt that because of working class racism and complacency, an insurrection would not begin unless it was led by Blacks, the only people who could fully appreciate both severe economic discrimination and racism.[70]

While in Cuba, he maintained that he was not a Communist and resisted the Party's attempts to force him into indoctrination courses. Williams felt that despite—or perhaps because of—his difficulties with the pro-Soviet faction, Castro supported him. This, he reasoned, was due to what Williams saw as a similar conflict between the Party stalwarts and Castro.[71] Williams consistently asserted that his sole task was to bring about Black liberation in the United States, not necessarily a proletariat revolution. He insisted on this distinction because, he felt, the abolition of capitalism in and of itself would not end the deeply embedded racism of the White workers. The ideal anti-racist, anti-imperialist America toward which he was struggling could be either capitalist or Communist in his view.[72]

Williams advocated armed self-defense among Blacks, referring back to Du Bois's recommendation of self-defense against White vigilante mobs. The young North Carolinian first became involved as a teenager in issues of community defense[73] and started a National Rifle Association gun club and an intelligence network in 1956 to protect his community against the Ku Klux Klan (KKK). A U.S. military veteran, he established training facilities where he and other former soldiers would train those without experience in combat. They soon amassed a cache of over 600 weapons.[74] As racial violence against Blacks in the South mounted, Williams advocated that his people prepare to launch urban guerrilla warfare in self-defense.[75]

Asserting that Afro-Americans were the vanguard of the world Black Revolution, he put forth his concepts of quick, intense campaigns in highly concentrated and sensitive urban areas that would spread to the countryside. Williams proposed a dual front consisting of an urban campaign in the North moving to a semi-urban effort in the South and then quickly switching to mobile warfare. He called for an organized Black Liberation Front, a Black general strike, an organized youth army and a system of developing cadres.[76]

Williams' tactics were obviously in direct contradiction to the dominant nonviolent philosophy at the time. His adamant support of armed self-defense created an internal split within the NAACP. He was temporarily suspended from the organization, but many still supported his views in spite of this official chastisement.[77] Putting aside their differences in tactics and views on the Cuban Revolution, Williams maintained that the NAACP had a place in the struggle for Black rights. Although criticized by mainstream organizations of the Civil Rights struggle, he won the support of the fringe elements; Malcolm X praised him as being "the first brother to take up arms and fight."[78]

Once in exile, Williams was eager to discuss the militant tactics outlined in his book *Theory of Urban Warfare*. However, the pro-Soviet faction was unwilling to entertain a public discussion of his tactics and constantly discouraged his militancy in private.[79] However, his reception by the Guevarist camp, or "Revolutionary Communists" in his terminology, was quite different. During Williams' visit to Cuba in 1960, Castro expressed his agreement with Williams' tactics and thanked him for his active support of the Cuban Revolution.[80] His tactics and militant stance against the U.S. government also won the support of Guevara, albeit too late for Che to affect Cuba's relations with the U.S. Movement. Throughout his exile in Cuba, Williams maintains, the most revolutionary members of the 26th of July Movement, including Guevara and Castro, continued to support his ideological and tactical stance.[81]

MALCOLM X

The time period separating Malcolm X's departure from the Nation of Islam and his assassination in 1965 was very brief: He officially announced his break with the organization on 8 March 1964 and was assassinated 21 February 1965. Therefore, throughout most of his political career, he extolled the ideas of Elijah Muhammad, which included a separatist philosophy of breaking away from the United States and forming a new Black Islamic country. The Nation of Islam did not support the Civil Rights struggle nor any other "reformist" or "integrationist" battles occurring at the time. In fact, the Nation was in many ways a de-politicizing force in the community, since members were not allowed to vote or run for official office. The organization also refused to work with non-Blacks in coalitions.

Malcolm's perspectives changed markedly, however, after his journey throughout the Middle East and Africa in 1964. Upon his return, he advocated viewing the U.S. Black struggle as part of the international fight against imperialist domination of the West over the Third World. He rejected the separatist ideas of the Nation of Islam and, instead, began to support political alliances in Black civil rights and self-defense.

Given the enmeshing of Malcolm's fluid spiritual development with his politicization process, it is difficult to define neatly his brand of nationalism. Stemming from the influence of his father's and Elijah Muhammad's beliefs in the pro-Africa tenets of Marcus Garvey, Malcolm displayed many characteristics of a Pan-Africanist. He was also an Islamic and African purist and a separatist from White mainstream culture, and thus, a cultural nationalist. Finally, his vehement calls to destroy the U.S. racist establishment and his advocating armed self-defense suggested a revolutionary nationalist platform.

Whatever the exact characterization of Malcolm's nationalism, his later concession to work with Whites, along with his leadership ability, his conclusion that armed struggle was necessary to overthrow the U.S. racist and imperialist power structure, and his understanding of the international character of the struggle, won him praise and support from the Guevarists within Cuba. In addition to the much publicized meeting in New York between Malcolm and Fidel in 1960, a lesser known display of solidarity occurred four years later between the Black Muslim and Guevara. While visiting the United Nations in 1964, Guevara had also planned to address an audience of Malcolm's. At the last minute citing security concerns, he was unable to attend, but sent a letter of apology which Malcolm read aloud to the audience. In the note, Guevara pledged Cuban solidarity with the U.S. Black struggle and pointed out their common goal of fighting for a free Africa.[82]

As a prominent Nation of Islam leader, Malcolm embraced the beliefs of racial superiority of Blacks and the characterization of Whites, including Jews, as "devils" who would eventually be destroyed by Allah.[83] Upon his disillusionment and eventual break with Elijah Muhammad, he sought to create an organization that would encompass the faiths of all Black people and therefore founded the Muslim Mosque, Inc. and the Organization of Afro-American Unity (OAAU), a political organization, in 1964.

After returning from his travels through the Middle East and African countries, he preached an even more conciliatory attitude toward all races. He revised his separatist philosophy after experiencing genuine brotherhood among Muslims of all colors.[84] Malcolm stated that his conversion to the "true" Islam had shown him his error in thinking that all Whites were intrinsically evil, and that, "it is a crass error to classify the revolution of the Negro as if it were a simple racial conflict between Negroes and whites or an exclusively U.S. problem. It is rather a worldwide rebellion of the exploited against the exploiters."[85]

For most of his political life, Malcolm viewed the world through a rigid racial paradigm. The Nation of Islam encouraged capitalist self-sufficiency of the Black race, and therefore class antagonisms were downplayed. Nevertheless, like Garvey, Malcolm connected with the underprivileged community of the Black ghetto. Around the time of his split with Elijah Muhammad, his ideology also took on an anti-capitalist slant.

He pointed to the Cuban, Vietnamese, and Chinese revolutions as examples to be emulated in the United States. This was quite a departure from his former stance and was well received by both factions within the Cuban regime. Furthermore, a Black Panther leader affirmed that Malcolm had planned to visit Cuba in March of 1965, the month after his assassination, in order to become more familiar with the Revolution.[86]

Because of the brevity of time that Malcolm had in which to develop his new thinking before his assassination, the Cubans did not become completely familiar with his ideological change until after he was gone. But, in the months and years that have followed his death, Malcolm's ideas have become the most widely read of any U.S. Black leader in Cuban history. The respect for his philosophy and accomplishments culminated in an international conference held in May 1990 that reflected upon his legacy on the twenty-fifth anniversary of his death.

In direct contrast to the mainstream teachings of King and other Civil Rights leaders, Malcolm maintained that Blacks would never win their freedom "non-violently, patiently and lovingly,"[87] and rather called on his people to take lessons in the strategy and tactics of self-defense in order to counter the KKK's violence.[88] Throughout the 1960s, the Cuban press, often echoing the Guevarist ideology, heralded the leadership of Malcolm as a long-awaited alternative to the "dangerously misguided" integrationist movement. They applauded his position on armed struggle and expressed the faction's hopes that U.S. Blacks were rejecting the pacifist philosophy which was allegedly financed by imperialists and were refusing to adopt a conciliatory stance which would only further their oppression.[89] However, it became increasingly clear to radical Black leaders who managed to visit Cuba around the time of Malcolm's death that the militant position voiced in the press was less and less representative of top Cuban leadership's hopes and plans for the Black Movement.

STOKELY CARMICHAEL

Stokely Carmichael began his ascension to national leadership within the Student Non-violent Coordinating Committee (SNCC), an organization founded in the South in 1960 and dedicated to the struggle for integration and civil rights. Initially based on the philosophical and religious ideal of nonviolence as put forth by King and others, SNCC, under the new direction of Carmichael, had moved in a more militant direction by 1966. Carmichael's radical faction continued to distance itself from King and the SCLC, saying that they were overly cautious in their tactics and unrealistic in their faith in White America.

As Carmichael developed his Black Power doctrine along Pan-Africanist lines, he began attempting to apply the ideology to the U.S. situation. Just as Pan-Africanists in Africa were telling sympathetic Whites to go back to Europe to fight in the core of the "empire," he was telling White U.S. sympathizers to return to their own communities to fight for Black rights there. Purges of White SNCC members ensued, since Carmichael also came to believe that each race should work within segregated organizations. His involvement with the revolutionary nationalist Black Panther Party in 1967 was ephemeral, since allegedly he could not bear working with Whites in coalitions, and the Panthers would not tolerate his using the Party name to propagate, in the words of Cleaver, "his racist cultural politics."[90] In January 1969, Carmichael left the United States for self-imposed exile in Conakry, Republic of Guinea, West Africa, where he continued to promote Pan-Africanism.

During his political career in the United States, Carmichael moved from a peaceful integrationist doctrine to positions of cultural nationalism, revolutionary nationalism within Black Power, and finally Pan-Africanism. The most radical definition of Black Power connoted both cultural and revolutionary nationalism, whereby Blacks would construct a movement to destroy all that Western civilization had created.[91] It had its roots in Garveyism and the thinking of Du Bois and stood for militant Black Nationalism, racial assertiveness, pride in African and diasporan culture and spirituality, and racial separatism.[92]

Carmichael adopted the tenets of Pan-Africanism late in the decade. As his disillusionment with coalition work and the insidiousness of U.S. racism grew, he embraced Pan-Africanism for its ideas of uniting all Africans in struggle for the decolonization of Africa and fighting apartheid and discrimination throughout the African world. Toward the end of Carmichael's tenure as a national leader of Blacks in the U.S., he more vehemently advocated the emigration of Blacks back to Africa to struggle for its decolonization. In this, he drew upon the history of Martin R. Delaney in the 1850s, who saw as the only solution for U.S. Blacks a return to Africa, and upon the platform of Marcus Garvey a century later.

The Cuban leadership—both the traditional Communist Party and the Guevarists—were disappointed with Carmichael's political growth toward Pan-Africanism.[93] The pro-Moscow contingent disliked his abandoning of his pacifist, Civil Rights roots, for they thought that he, more than anyone else, had the potential of replacing King as a more militant mainstream leader. The Guevarists were encouraged by his turn toward advocating armed struggle and fighting against imperialism worldwide but regretted his increasingly hostile stance toward Whites.

Carmichael was accused of holding racist views not only by supporters of Black rights within the White community but also other Black Nationalist leaders. His campaign to purge White members from the originally integrated SNCC organization was seen by many as racially prejudiced. Panther leader Huey P. Newton accused him of propagating "pork chop nationalism," a reactionary form of cultural nationalism which was anti-socialist in its orientation and strove to oppress others. Carmichael, however, defended his segregationist position as a necessary measure for political survival. Based on the history of betrayal, co-optation and infiltration of the Black struggle by Whites, he asserted, "there is, in fact, no group at present with whom to form a coalition in which Blacks will not be absorbed and betrayed."[94]

Initially, Carmichael's platform seemed to embody both a class and a race analysis, similar to that held by the Black Panther Party. He recognized that racism, economic exploitation and cultural integrity must all be addressed equally. Constant throughout were his anti-capitalist, anti-imperialist and pro-land reform ideals, similar to those of Castro in the wake of taking power in Cuba. Nonetheless, as he moved closer to a Pan-Africanist ideology in the second half of the decade, the issue of race came to dominate his analysis.

The Cuban regime, not yet aware of Carmichael's full embrace of a race perspective, gave him a grand reception as a guest at the Organization of Latin American Solidarity (OLAS) convention in 1967. The Cuban media confidently hailed Carmichael as the vanguard minority leader continuing to develop Malcolm's thinking and action along the correct path from "a race consciousness to a colonialized consciousness." This vanguard, assured the Cuban media, was "against discrimination and underdevelopment, not against the whites as such."[95]

Although publicly demonstrating his solidarity with the regime by stating, "we share with you a common struggle . . . we have a common enemy. Our enemy is white western society,"[96] privately he voiced concerns over Cuban racism. Upon leaving the OLAS convention for Africa and Europe, Carlos Moore discussed Carmichael's hesitations about the regime with him. His issues were similar to those voiced by Williams earlier in the decade and centered on the fact that Blacks were not in positions of real power.[97] The following year, Carmichael attempted to dissuade Cleaver from seeking exile in Cuba because of "Cuban racism."[98]

That same year, Carmichael declared that socialism and Communism were irrelevant to Black Power because they did not deal sufficiently with the most important issue of racism. He criticized these ideologies for focusing on class exploitation, which Carmichael thought should be secondary.[99] Not long after, in 1969, Carmichael commented that, although he had read very little of Marx and had not understood that which he had read, all struggles needed a land base and therefore all Africans everywhere in the world, including African Americans, should first engage in armed struggle *in Africa* in order to take back a White-ruled country.[100]

Upon seeking self-imposed exile in Africa that year, however, Carmichael once again took on both a race and a class perspective. In a compilation of his speeches assembled in 1971, he chose to edit the above-mentioned passage denouncing Communism from his "Declaration of War," claiming that at the time he had not explained clearly that he meant "the sterile, stale brand of European Marxism-Leninism which so many 'white radicals' in [the U.S.] were trying to push on Black activists."[101]

From that time forward, Carmichael continued to refer to Castro, Guevara and the Cuban Revolution in a positive manner. Speaking in

Atlanta in April 1970 in the context of explaining Marx's theory that individuals of the bourgeoisie will turn away from their class to join the proletariat, he said, "Fidel is an example of this—he was a member of the aristocracy, he betrayed his class interests, joined the masses and led a successful revolution."[102]

Within a few short years, Carmichael's views on tactical violence changed considerably from his original nonviolent stance within SNCC. He was a front-runner among the militant wing of the Civil Rights Movement who eventually would yield, en masse, to Malcolm and Williams' call for armed self-defense. By the late 1960s, Carmichael followed in the steps of Williams in his progression toward accepting not only armed self-defense, but also revolutionary violence to achieve Black liberation worldwide. The Guevarist faction within the Cuban government and press were in full agreement with Carmichael's changing tactical stance; however, when he turned to Pan-Africanism in the late decade, Carmichael and the Cubans temporarily diverged.

Carmichael, like Williams, foresaw that the struggle would begin in the cities, not in the country as the theory of the guerrilla "foco" maintained. But this difference did not prevent Carmichael from considering Che's experience a great example. In a statement upon Guevara's death in 1967 that Carmichael requested to have disseminated on Cuban radio and in the printed press, he pointed to Che's final letter to the *Tricontinental* as a guide for Blacks in the United States and for all revolutionaries throughout the world. Carmichael explained that Che, like Malcolm, knew that the time for talk had passed and the time was *now* to fight. As with Malcolm's death, he predicted that the murder of Guevara would spawn a new group of fighters who would realize their duty as revolutionaries to "create Vietnams inside the United States."[103]

That same year, the regime's official news organization, *Granma*, printed a statement that validated the U.S. Black militant's idea of urban struggle. In the statement, members of the Cuban Committee of Solidarity with South Vietnam, on the Day of Solidarity with the North American Black Struggle, declared Carmichael's plan of Black Power to be correct. The committee predicted that the ghettos of the big cities would be turned into *focos revolucionarios* (revolutionary focal points) in the heart of imperialism.[104]

Shortly after King's assassination on 4 April 1968, Carmichael appeared in the Cuban press claiming that the death of the pacifist leader signified the death of the philosophy of nonviolent struggle and proved that revolutionary violence was necessary.[105] He charged that White America had made a mistake in killing King, because thereafter there would be no one to tell Blacks not to burn the cities. Announcing that major urban guerrilla warfare would ensue, he asserted that King's death "means we've gone full swing into the Revolution," and pledged to give his life to the cause.[106] In a letter of condolence to King's family, the Havana-based Organization of Solidarity with the Peoples of Africa, Asia, and Latin America (OSPAAAL) reiterated that his death would mark the turning point of the Movement by leading to "total confrontation."[107]

ELDRIDGE CLEAVER

Eldridge Cleaver spent most of the Civil Rights era behind bars in California. Despite that, he took sides in this struggle by joining the Nation of Islam in proclaiming voluntary segregation as the correct way forward for African Americans. As the split between Malcolm X and Elijah Muhammad deepened, however, Cleaver sided with Malcolm in his more conciliatory stance toward the Civil Rights struggle and coalition work with non-Blacks. Largely self-educated by reading the works of revolutionaries throughout history, Cleaver, upon his release from prison, was prepared to work with White liberals and the proletariat toward achieving a Black-led revolution.

Cleaver joined the Black Panther Party for Self-Defense in 1967 as their Minister of Information. The Party, founded by Huey P. Newton and Bobby Seale a year earlier, possessed a revolutionary nationalist platform. Their program, entitled "What we Want Now! What we Believe," boldly asserted that Blacks would not be free until they were able to determine their own destiny. It maintained that government has the responsibility to guarantee full employment and if this responsibility was not met, "then the means of production should be taken from the business men and placed in the community." The Panthers further demanded land redistribution, state cooperatives, free housing and education aimed at "knowledge of self." Party members refused to fight in what they deemed racist wars waged against other people of color and proposed instead to mobilize Black self-defense groups in order to halt police violence and, moreover, to fully arm the Black population for this purpose. Finally, they pointed out the legal right of the people to end a government that has become destructive to the liberties of its citizens.[108]

Cleaver and the Party leadership drew their inspiration from Du Bois, Garvey, Franz Fanon, and Malcolm X. In fact, Cleaver identified completely with the program of Malcolm X, considering him his personal leader, and patterned many of his own activities after Malcolm's example. But Cleaver and the other Panther leaders also looked to Guevara as a role model for his views on nationalism, internationalism, culture and humanity. They recognized that Che was not promoting the violent dissolution of all nations but rather self-determination as a right for each group of people. They believed that each community should reflect its cultural heritage and that, in the future, culture would play an integral role in establishing foreign policy in what chief Panther theoretician Newton saw to be a "Nation of Nations," or the post-struggle United States. For the Panthers, to understand Che's idea of internationalism was to understand the dialectical integration of nationalism and internationalism.[109]

They saw Guevara's views as a direct contradiction to the incorrect position held by cultural nationalists. The Panthers maintained that this strain of nationalist could not comprehend why Whites would turn against the system, and thus could not accept their assistance. They criticized this "reactionary" nationalism as an anti-socialist perspective which had as its end the oppression of others.[110] Newton and Cleaver, like the Cubans, held that culture itself would not liberate African Americans and that a reversion to African culture would not bring about political freedom. The united struggle, they insisted, should be waged against both capitalism and racism and should be led by a socialist revolutionary party.

Cleaver, like Newton, directly challenged the institutionalized racism around him and actively worked to dispel reactionary racism from himself and his party. The Panthers were willing to collaborate with White progressives, acknowledged that the idea of "culture" was fluid, and upheld both revolutionary Black Nationalism and a class consciousness as the correct perspective for U.S. Blacks. Although they maintained, as had Malcolm, that their own Party must first be entirely Black in order to create internal unity, the Panthers had been working with White progressives since their earliest days and saw that these "children of the beast" were seeking new heroes in the Black leaders. The Panther Party commented that these Whites were turning away from their slave-owning heroes and had to choose their ally, "Lyndon Baines Johnson or Fidel Castro."[111] As a Party leader, Cleaver pledged his support for all people who were struggling for self-determination, regardless of color.[112]

The Panthers were the closest ideological fit with the Guevarist faction during the Nationalist stage of the U.S. struggle. They were supportive of the Cuban Revolution, propagated a Marxist-Leninist ideology and were involved in alliances with White progressives. In fact, according to Amuchastegui, it was White liberals—mainly from the Students for a Democratic Society (SDS) and scholars from California universities—who first brought the Panthers to the attention of the Cuban leadership in 1967. These White intellectuals brought Black Panther Party literature and Cleaver's book *Soul On Ice* to Havana for the Cubans to read.[113]

Cleaver and the Panthers also subscribed to the Guevarist conviction that society could not make a transition to socialism within a capitalist state. Therefore, the fight must be waged against the common enemy of humanity, "U.S. imperialism and all the running dogs."[114] This belligerent position, however, was deemed excessively risky and therefore was not well received among the traditional Cuban Communists who dominated the government late in the decade.

Another point of contention with the pro-Moscow camp was Cleaver's vocal, ideological kinship with the Chinese rather than the USSR, which was the same position as that of the debilitated Guevarists. The Chinese model of a peasant-based revolution was more in line with the Panthers' way of thinking; indeed, they called themselves "techno-peasants," i.e. peasants who happen to be displaced in large urban areas. They also identified strongly with the *lumpen proletariat* (that is, in modern Western terminology, the unemployed masses on the government dole), whereas the pro-Soviet stalwarts followed Marx in stigmatizing the lumpen class. The Panthers drew much of their support from this class and identified them as the left-wing of the proletariat and the most revolutionary segment because they were the most desperate.

Upon departing from Cuba in 1969, Cleaver further developed this concept of the importance of the lumpen class. In his own form of neo-Marxism, he theorized that the lumpen proletariat, largely Black, was the only class capable of rising up and overthrowing the White capitalist system. The goal, he asserted, was to achieve equality of *distribution* and *consumption*, not equality of ownership in the means of production, which he concluded to be a crucial error in Marx's original analysis.[115]

Another ideological sticking point with the pro-Soviets was Cleaver's belief—along with the Guevarists and Fanon—that in each country the socialist revolution would be unique and that therefore the Marxian model must be adapted to the situation and not strictly imposed upon the current reality. Since the nature of class distinctions is different in each country, a strict reading of Marx's prescriptions for the European proletariat was not deemed sufficient for most contemporary world struggles. Cleaver came to this conclusion through his study of philosophy, Asian religion, Jungian psychology and Joseph Campbell's writings on mass movements. This enabled him to analyze the structures of foreign ideologies and conclude that they could not be applied to the United States.[116] He, like Fanon, Malcolm, and Carmichael, saw that a race analysis must be added to the class analysis when looking at colonial societies and economies.

The revolutionary violence advocated by Cleaver and his party envisioned an urban-based assault led by a Black revolutionary vanguard. These vanguard fighters would teach by setting examples for action. The Party saw itself as the guerrilla leaders of the coming insurrection, because its members understood the theories and ideology of struggle. They viewed the guerrilla not only as a warrior in the literal sense but also as a military commander and political theoretician—the "perfect man"—who was embodied in the example of Che. Cleaver and the Panthers held that the guerrilla's role was to give the workers and peasants an education, because the guerrilla fighter was the "perfect unity of mind and body."[117]

The Panthers' affinity for unorthodox guerrilla fighting carried over to an ideological alliance with the most revolutionary elements in the Cuban leadership against those who claimed to be Communists yet would not eagerly assist their brand of revolutionary struggle. They shared Guevara's distaste for those Communist parties around the world that wanted to be the "mind" of the revolution or that wanted to control the action without participating in the practical work. They publicly condemned the Communist Party of Bolivia for failing to give Guevara sufficient support in his final attempt at insurrection.[118] However, what Cleaver did not divulge until years later was his own frustration with the Cuban Communist Party for treating U.S. Blacks in the same way that the Bolivians treated Che.

Former Cuban intelligence official Domingo Amuchastegui claims that the regime recognized at all times that the objective conditions for revolution in the United States did not exist, nor could they be forced by a small group of Black militants.[119] Cleaver disagrees and rebuts that those Cubans loyal to Guevara, including Castro, were hopeful that the Black vanguard could act as a catalyst for igniting the U.S. insurrection that would ultimately draw in the Anti-War Movement.[120]

His experience was corroborated by Williams' own conflicts with the "Bourgeois Communists" and convergence with the "Revolutionary Communists." Cleaver asserts that in all his dealings with the revolutionary Cubans, i.e. with the Guevarist faction, their shared ideology was an important part of the relationship. It is no surprise, then, that this faction had a great deal of respect for the Black Panther Party, particularly since both were in agreement on all major philosophical issues.[121]

As was the case with Robert Williams, however, in the opinion of the dominant pro-Soviet ideologues of the late 1960s, the Panthers' tactics of violence were better suited for Third World revolutionaries than for urban North Americans. This difference of opinion between competing ideologies eventually led to conflict. Throughout his exile, Cleaver was repeatedly dissuaded from his tactical line of thought and, instead, was offered suggestions as to where the Panthers' efforts could be channeled most successfully, namely, by putting down their weapons and linking their struggle with the broader Anti-War and workers' movements in order to force the U.S. government to change its interventionist policies.[122]

ANGELA DAVIS

Angela Yvonne Davis grew up in the segregated South just as the Civil Rights struggle was heating up. Her earliest political activism included taking part in the fight for integration, attending Civil Rights protests with her mother, canvassing for voter registration and attempting to organize interracial study groups in her school.[123] Her belief in integrated struggle began early and stayed with her throughout her career as Black militant and CPUSA leader.

The question of whether a member of the CPUSA could also be a Black nationalist is a difficult one to answer. Although faithful to her ideological Marxist-Leninist base, Davis often peppered her statements with proclamations of identity as a Black woman in struggle against the "white capitalist United States" which was oppressing people of color around the world. This may have been a tactical move in order to achieve the immediate objectives of inserting herself into the mainstream struggle and influencing the Black masses who were at the time swayed by nationalism. At the same time, she could have maintained her Marxist-Leninist strategy of mass action that would lead to insurrection and the eventual dictatorship of the proletariat. In any case, her simultaneous involvement with SNCC, the Black Panther Party, and the CPUSA's Che-Lumumba Club (an all-Black Marxist-Leninist collective) demonstrated the grey area between nationalism and Marxism in which many Black activists dwelt in the 1960s.

Although opposed by many CPUSA stalwarts, the Che-Lumumba Club was an attempt to bring Black Power followers, Pan-Africanists and revolutionary nationalists into the Communist fold. The group dealt with issues such as segregation and police brutality, and the discussion often turned nationalistic and anti-White in tone. Prominent CPUSA leader Dorothy Healey felt that Davis may very well have not joined the Party if not for the fluid treatment of nationalism and class struggle in the Che-Lumumba collective.[124]

Davis was not so much a Black revolutionary nationalist as a revolutionary *internationalist*. She thought that the position of revolutionary nationalists advocating the strategy of Black-led insurrection was dangerously misguided, ultimately destructive in nature, and would only lead to a worsening of the situation for Blacks. Rather, she held that only a multi-ethnic, class-based political—not necessarily violent—struggle led by Blacks would bring about the successful transfer of the wealth and riches of the country into the hands of the producers, Black and White.[125] Her later criticism of Black Nationalism was that its proponents were unscientific in that they neglected what she saw as the primary causes of Black oppression: economic and class exploitation.[126]

A staunch anti-racist, Davis worked tirelessly within the CPUSA to purge it of its White chauvinism and insensitivity toward oppressed Party members and ethnic groups. Throughout the decade and beyond, Davis at times critiqued the racial myopia of her White comrades and at others praised the organization for its genuine efforts and accomplishments toward racial equality.[127]

Her willingness to address the racism of the CPUSA carried over to her international comrades as well. She was an avid supporter of the Cuban Revolution, highlighting both the accomplishments and the challenges that the Cubans faced, including the struggle to eradicate the prerevolutionary vestiges of racism from Cuban society. In her inspection of the nascent revolution, Davis learned a valuable lesson about the need to battle racism relentlessly "at all times and at all levels." She found that although the overall status of Afro-Cubans had improved, residual racism still persisted into the end of the first decade after the insurrection.[128]

Davis's introduction to a class perspective began with her study of Marxist philosophy at Brandeis University. This experience helped her to see the Black struggle in the context of the larger proletarian struggle worldwide.[129] Her subsequent graduate study in Frankfurt, Germany, crystallized Davis's class analysis of struggle. She returned to the United States in 1967, and in June 1968 formally joined the CPUSA and became active in the Che-Lumumba Club.[130]

Her decision to join the Communist Party was made in accordance with her strong conviction that the only correct road to Black liberation was that which pointed toward the complete overthrow of the U.S. capitalist class and structure. Davis adopted a class analysis almost out of necessity, as it were, since she was convinced that, as a minority group, Blacks would literally be committing suicide by trying to challenge U.S. capitalism on their own; therefore they needed the help of Marxists everywhere to destroy the system that by definition oppressed Blacks.[131]

But her perspective was not exclusively based on class; rather, like other nationalist leaders, she viewed the issue of race as inextricable from the contemporary U.S. struggle. Given the all-pervasive nature of racism in U.S. society, regardless of class, Davis concluded that Black leadership was necessary at the head of the popular struggle toward socialism: "black-white unity with black people in the forefront."[132]

Davis saw it as absolutely essential that Whites actively fight racism and accept Blacks as the leaders in the struggle. She contended that only in this way could Whites liberate themselves of their racist paralysis and take part in radical agitation. Blacks, on the other hand, responding to their own oppression under racism, had become increasingly revolutionary in philosophy and militant in their behavior, and thus were the natural leaders for the mass action.[133] By agitating at all levels, eventually Blacks would help to build a socialist society that would liberate not only African Americans but all the world's oppressed peoples.[134]

After being wrongly jailed for kidnapping, conspiracy and murder in 1970, Davis commented, "All the socialist countries have lodged protests [against her incarceration] in some way or form. I was particularly pleased to hear of the activity that has been going on in Cuba."[135] Thanks to her ideological stance in support of class struggle and against minority-waged insurrection, the Communist stalwarts influencing Cuban policy late in the decade were quick to support Davis in her quest for freedom.

Davis advocated a mass-based proletarian struggle, political in nature and without a military strategy of revolutionary violence. Her main concern with Williams' or the Black Panther Party's position on revolutionary violence was that their focus of activity was based on military strategy alone—that is, guerrilla warfare—rather than on a political strategy that *might* employ military tactics in a subordinate role at some time in the future. Davis concurred to a large extent with the official CPUSA position against these types of nationalists, which was that they were putschist, irresponsible provocateurs. Their actions were seen as feeding the persecution of the Black masses and the Left and as giving the U.S. government an excuse to build up an oppressive machinery against all progressives regardless of their rejection or acceptance of violent tactics.

NOTES

1. José Luis Llovio-Menéndez, *Insider: My Hidden Life as a Revolutionary in Cuba* (New York: Bantam Books, 1988), 129.
2. A. Díaz, "Balance de la actividad de la Dirección Nacional del Partido desde el 26 de julio hasta la fecha" [Assessment of the Activity of the Party National Leadership since 26 July until Today], *Fundamentos* (Havana) (May 1954); 111–13, 133–37, reprinted in chapter 13 "The Cuban Revolution," Michael Löwy, ed., *Marxism in Latin America from 1909 to the Present* (Atlantic Highlands, N.J.: Humanities Press International, Inc., 1992), 153.
3. Goldenberg, 167.
4. Llovio-Menéndez, 82–83.
5. Louis A. Pérez, Jr., *Cuba: Between Reform and Revolution* (New York: Oxford University Press, 1995), 320–23.
6. Cohen, 208. While in this particular case Piñeiro was asserting the Communist Party line, it is fair to say that many Cuban scholars argue that Piñeiro, far from being a Soviet ideologue, was more a yes-man for Castro's security dictates. Williams and Cleaver, who both interacted with Piñeiro, were apparently not fully aware of his alleged connection with Castro and felt that he was in the pro-Soviet camp; they clearly saw Fidel as more sympathetic to their views.
7. Ibid., 290.
8. Amuchastegui, interview.
9. Cohen, 278.
10. Ibid., 315.
11. Ibid., 218.
12. Llovio-Menéndez, 114.
13. Rojo, 92.
14. Ibid., 61.

15. Ernesto "Che" Guevara, "Internationalism and Anti-imperialism," *Tricontinental*, no. 2 (September-October 1967): 12.
16. Ibid., 27.
17. Ibid., 20.
18. Ibid., 17.
19. Rojo, 94.
20. Cohen, 276.
21. Ibid.
22. Regis Debray, *Revolution in the Revolution?* (New York: Monthly Review Press, 1967).
23. Fidel Castro, "Fidel at the Closing of OLAS," *Granma*, 20 August 1967, 3.
24. Rojo, 140.
25. Guevara, "Internationalism," 31.
26. Castro, "Fidel at OLAS," 3.
27. Ibid., 4.
28. Guevara, "Internationalism," 5.
29. See Fidel Castro, "Statement by Fidel Castro at the Solemn Tribute in Havana," *Tricontinental* no. 2 (September-October 1967): 111.
30. "USA: From Little Rock to Urban Rebellions," *Tricontinental Bulletin*, no. 46 (January 1970): 16.
31. Ernesto "Che" Guevara, *Venceremos! The Speeches and Writings of Ernesto Che Guevara*, ed. John Gerassi (New York: Simon and Schuster, 1968), 378–86.
32. Quoted in Llovio-Menéndez, 114.
33. Cohen, 292.
34. In Lee Lockwood, *Castro's Cuba, Cuba's Fidel* (New York: Vintage Books, 1969), 81.
35. Amuchastegui, interview.
36. Pérez, 321.
37. Ibid., 315.
38. Franqui, 473.
39. Pérez, 321.
40. Jorge I. Domínguez, *Cuba: Order and Revolution* (Cambridge: Harvard University Press, 1978), 485.
41. Cleaver, interview.
42. Moore's interview with Franqui, in Moore, 37–38.
43. Cleaver, interview; and Stokely Carmichael, letter to author, 8 October 1995.
44. Goldenberg, 167.
45. Suchlicki, 52–57.
46. Goldenberg, 340.
47. Fidel Castro, in *Bohemia* (Havana), 23 December 1966.
48. Fidel Castro, "Fidel: Quienes no sean combatientes revolucionarios no puedan llamarse comunistas" [Fidel: Those who are not revolutionary fighters cannot be called Communists], *Granma*, 14 March 1967, 3d ed.
49. Fidel Castro, in *Granma*, 15 May 1966.

50. Castro, "Fidel at OLAS," 3.

51. Cleaver, interview; Moore, 273; and Rojo, 191.

52. Martin Luther King, Jr., *Stride Toward Freedom* (Harper & Row, 1986), back cover.

53. In Sheila Bernard and Sam Pollard, "The Time has Come," *Eyes on the Prize, II* (Boston: Blackside, Inc., 1990).

54. White, 120.

55. From King's FBI File dated 22 July 1964, in Earl Ofari Hutchinson, *Blacks and Reds: Race and Class in Conflict, 1919-1990* (East Lansing: Michigan State University Press, 1995), 269.

56. Ibid.

57. White, 117.

58. Ibid., 14.

59. Ibid., 133.

60. Ibid., 135.

61. Amuchastegui, interview.

62. Ibid.

63. White, 136.

64. Cohen, 333.

65. Ibid., 247.

66. Ibid., 344.

67. Ibid., 272.

68. Ibid., 271.

69. Ibid., 33.

70. Ibid., 208.

71. Ibid., 229.

72. Ibid., 220–21.

73. Ibid., 25.

74. Ibid., 97–99.

75. Ibid., 271.

76. Max Stanford, "Black Guerrilla Warfare: Strategy and Tactics," *Black Scholar* (November 1970): 31–35.

77. Cohen, 111–31.

78. Ibid., 132.

79. Amuchastegui, interview.

80. Cohen, 143.

81. Ibid., 228.

82. Moore, 189–90.

83. Malcolm X, *Malcolm X Speaks: Selected Speeches and Statements*, ed. George Breitman (New York: Pathfinder Press, 1989), 5–16.

84. Ibid., 162–63, 198.

85. Edmundo Desnoes, "The Negro Movement in the United States: NOW," *Granma*, 7 January 1968, 11.

86. George Murray and Joudon Major Ford, "Black Panthers: the Afro-Americans' Challenge," interview in *Tricontinental* (January-February 1969): 109.

87. Malcolm X, "USA: The Hour of Mau Mau," *Tricontinental*, no. 11 (March-April 1969): 29.

88. Ibid., 30.

89. See, for example, *Tricontinental Bulletin*, no. 43 (October 1969): 31–32.

90. Cleaver, interview.

91. Glickman, 49.

92. White, 13.

93. Amuchastegui, interview.

94. Stokely Carmichael, *Stokely Speaks: Black Power to Pan-Africanism* (New York: Random House, 1971.

95. Desnoes, 11.

96. Carmichael, *Stokely Speaks*, editor's preface.

97. Moore, 260–61.

98. Cleaver, interview.

99. Moore, 261.

100. Stokely Carmichael, "Pan-Africanism—Land and Power," *Black Scholar* (November 1969): 36–43.

101. Carmichael, *Stokely Speaks*, xvi.

102. Ibid.

103. Stokely Carmichael, "This is Not the Time for Tears but for Combat, States Carmichael in Message on the Death of Che Guevara," *Granma*, 26 November 1967, 11.

104. R. Casals, "En Watts inició la lucha armada del pueblo afroamericano" [In Watts the Armed Struggle of the Afroamerican People Began], *Granma*, 18 August 1967, 6.

105. Stokely Carmichael, "Carmichael Comments on the Slaying of Martin Luther King and the Struggle of U.S. Black People," *Granma*, 21 April 1968, 11.

106. Ibid.

107. "OSPAAAL's Message to SNCC," *Granma*, 21 April 1968, 11.

108. Huey P. Newton and Bobby Seale, "The Black Panther," in *Black Nationalism in America*, ed. John H. Bracey, Jr., August Meier, and Elliott Rudwick, (New York: The Bobbs-Merrill Company, Inc., 1970), 4.

109. Huey P. Newton, "Culture and Liberation," *Tricontinental*, no. 11 (March-April 1969): 101–4.

110. Huey P. Newton, "Black Power and the Revolutionary Struggle," *Tricontinental Bulletin*, no. 32 (November 1968): 5.

111. Ibid., 8–9.

112. Ibid., 12.

113. Amuchastegui, interview.

114. Huey P. Newton, "Culture and Liberation," 101–4.

115. Eldridge Cleaver, "On Lumpen Ideology," *The Black Scholar* (November–December 1972): 2–10.
116. Cleaver, interview.
117. Huey P. Newton, "Black Power," 12.
118. Ibid.
119. Amuchastegui, interview.
120. Cleaver, interview.
121. Ibid.
122. Ibid.; and Amuchastegui, interview.
123. Angela Yvonne Davis, *If They Come in the Morning: Voices of Resistance* (New York: Third Press, 1971), 171; and Anne Janette Johnson, "Angela Davis," in *Contemporary Black Biography* (Detroit: Gale Research, Inc., 1992), 74.
124. Hutchinson, 281.
125. Davis, *If They Come in the Morning*, 181.
126. Mary Frances Berry and John W. Blassingame, *Long Memory—The Black Experience in America* (New York: Oxford University Press, 1982), 423.
127. Hutchinson, 297.
128. Davis, *If They Come in the Morning*, 179.
129. Johnson, 74.
130. Ibid., 75.
131. Davis, *If They Come in the Morning*, 180.
132. Ibid., 182.
133. Ibid.
134. Ibid., 180.
135. Ibid., 177.

ISSUES OF SECURITY

The two conflicting views over the issue of security—both Cuba's national security and Black leaders' individual safety—sprang from the fundamental divergence in ideologies of the Guevarist camp versus the pro-Soviet, traditional Communists. The nature of relations with the U.S. Black Movement depended on which faction was influencing Castro directly and which held positions of power with the ability to set policy independently.

As the decade progressed, Cuban policy toward the U.S. Movement was inconsistent and thus confusing for African Americans. A useful way to view these fluctuations, then, is by the ascent and descent within the Cuban power structure of the two camps. By the second half of the decade, Castro was either seduced by, or unable to halt, the conservative pro-Moscow influence over security policy in Cuba.

The issue of Cuban national security should be thought of as economic stability as well as the ability to prevent or withstand outside attack or internal counterrevolution. It necessitated either searching for rapprochement with the United States, bargaining with the USSR and China for the best comprehensive security pledges that would still allow a degree of independence, or embarking on a totally new path. The conflicting camps were polarized over these issues by mid-decade.

THE GUEVARIST FACTION

The Guevarist approach to ensuring Cuba's national security held that in order to achieve economic and political independence for all the nations of

Latin America, the forceful overthrow of the current capitalist and neo-colonial governments had to be actively supported. A revolution in a country with a large economy, such as Venezuela, Argentina or Brazil, was desperately needed if an independent, socialist Cuba were to survive in the face of increasing isolation. This isolation was due mainly to direct and indirect maneuverings by the United States and to policies of the Castro government that antagonized the U.S. and Cuba's former allies in Latin America and elsewhere.

Guevara did not seem to make a distinction between the Third and the First World (namely the United States) when supporting insurrection. To him, Cuban security would be ensured by promoting revolution everywhere. And, as we shall see, his strict adherence to this security policy was the primary reason for his forced departure from power in Cuba. Although the idea of a revolution in the United States in the early 1960s seemed remote, Guevara did not rule it out and rather considered it a possibility as long as U.S. Blacks united in violent protest and the working class mobilized in support.[1] In Guevara's view, if revolution was to be fueled anywhere it sprang up, then flames of unrest in the "belly of the beast" surely had to be fanned, since U.S. intervention was Cuba's primary security concern.

It is reasonable to conclude that Castro supported Guevara's approach to Cuban security policy. A consummate politician, Castro seemed to cast Guevara (possibly with Che's initial approval) as a formidable "extremist" so as to allow himself some maneuvering room with the Soviets and with the traditional Communist Party forces within the regime, and to portray himself as the accommodationist among all parties involved. As U.S. and Soviet pressure grew throughout the decade and the space for maneuvering contracted, Castro could blame Guevara and his faction when violence failed and Che's (not Castro's) security policy yielded disappointing results. The deathblow to this policy, and perhaps Castro's final step away from the Guevarist faction, was dealt by Che's failed insurrectional attempt and ultimate execution in Bolivia.

Although initially trusting the USSR, Guevara soon understood that international solidarity and support for revolution were not primary considerations in the Soviets' national interests. Particularly after the 1962 Missile Crisis, Guevara grew more and more wary of heeding Moscow's advice. As his frustration grew, however, so too grew the influence of the pro-Soviet Communists in Cuba in establishing security policy.

TRADITIONAL COMMUNIST PARTY FACTION

The pro-Moscow faction took its guidance directly from the USSR and largely deferred policy decisions about relations with the United States and support for insurrectional struggles to the Kremlin. They believed in following the lead set by the Soviets toward peaceful coexistence with the West as the correct road to ensuring national security. Therefore, during the first stage of the early 1960s U.S. struggle, this faction publicly supported the pacifist Civil Rights leaders, since this stance would not threaten Soviet and Cuban attempts at rapprochement with Washington. Because this first stage was primarily domestic and not international in nature, no overtures were made between Havana and the mainstream Movement's most prominent leader, Martin Luther King, Jr. The relationship, the traditional Communist Party faction felt, should be one of mutual political support in terms of solidarity actions; these actions, however, were limited so as not to risk sending the message to the U.S. government of a Cuban attempt to meddle internally in U.S. affairs, a message that would risk retaliation.[2]

But when confronted with more militant U.S. Blacks advocating armed self-defense or insurrection, the pro-USSR faction recoiled. The radicalizing leadership of the Black Nationalist stage posed a much greater threat to the facade of "revolutionary internationalism" behind which the conservative leaders hid. Williams and others discovered that the "Bourgeois Communists" benefited from maintaining revolutionary rhetoric and official support of revolution. Without it their own people might either demand truly progressive leadership that would remain faithful to the precepts on which the Revolution was based or call for a return to a capitalist economy and society under which a decent standard of living could be obtained, since building the enlightened, socialist man would be exposed as a failure.[3]

The revolutionary slogans encouraging Third World insurgents to recognize that the only struggle for liberation is armed struggle could be heard throughout the streets of Havana and read in Cuban publications in the middle and late 1960s. Yet, the pro-Soviet-dominated government tried hard to avoid sending messages that would in any way suggest to the U.S. government that the regime was sponsoring violence on the part of the Black revolutionaries.[4]

Despite that effort, at times, Fidel, in a state of defiant nostalgia or frustration against what was becoming an increasingly bureaucratized and conservative government, would fire off revolutionary proclamations in support of U.S. Black insurrection. The combination of the official radical propaganda and Castro's passionate pleas led many to believe that Cuba would risk all for the U.S. Black revolution; but national security issues, from the perspective of the traditional Communist Party faction to which Castro increasingly subscribed, took precedence over the rhetorical revolutionary stance in the government's actual decision making.

THE STRUGGLE TO SET POLICY

The view of the role that the Black Movement could play in the growing Anti-War Movement, as well as the hoped-for outcome of the entire U.S. struggle, was quite different between the two Cuban camps. The pro-Soviets held that the objective conditions to begin an insurrection in the United States did not exist, nor could they be brought about by a small group of Black militants. Since struggle based on ethnicity was seen as divisive and illegitimate, the best that Black workers could do was be absorbed into the larger Anti-War and workers' struggle.[5] In this way, the traditional Communists hoped to force Washington's hand and compel the U.S. not to interfere in Cuban affairs.

But the experiences of Williams and Cleaver revealed that those within the regime who subscribed to Che's guerrilla "foco" theory as an international example were hopeful that the Black vanguard could ignite the largely White Anti-War Movement and push for radical change in the United States. The most idealistic hope was that an insurrection could take hold in the United States, led by those most oppressed, the African Americans.

The battle within the Cuban regime to define dominant policies first publicly surfaced when five ministers resigned in June 1959. Guevara consequently left Cuba on his first brief tour of Africa and Asia. Many interpreted this move as the result of pressure put on Castro to distance himself, at least temporarily, from Guevara, who was considered too far to the left.[6] But upon Che's return, Castro had, for the most part, consolidated his power, and was able to name Che head of the Ministry of Industry within the National Institute for Agrarian Reform (INRA) and soon after appointed him president of the National Bank of Cuba.[7] Guevara's growing importance signaled to the United States that Cuba was coming under the control of the most radical forces.[8] It also meant that the Guevarists, at least initially, had the upper hand in establishing an active security policy aimed at promoting revolution.

Dissimilar opinions of the relations between Cuba and the Nation of Islam also reveal the divergence of the two factions' security concerns and approaches to that issue. The traditional Communist Party elements argued that, although the Nation of Islam was gaining prominence in the U.S. Movement, its antigovernment position was too risky to support: "You don't play with Islam" for national security reasons, remembered Amuchastegui. In the case of the Muslims' most charismatic leader, Malcolm X, the pro-Soviets downplayed his meeting with Castro in New York in 1960 and pointed out that the two leaders had no further contact.[9]

On the other hand, Carlos Moore offers a different opinion: Throughout 1961, numerous attempts were allegedly made by Cuban intelligence to secure relations with the Nation of Islam and the Armed Deacons of Self-Defense (ADSD), a Black militant organization based in the South. He indicates that the Cuban government had been following with interest the progress of the Black Muslims since Fidel's meeting with Malcolm in Harlem. The Cuban mission to the United Nations repeatedly invited members of the Nation of Islam, and in particular Malcolm, to visit their country; Malcolm did not go, but Herbert Muhammad, the son of Elijah, was sent in 1963.[10] Such disparate attitudes suggest that from the beginning of the decade, each Cuban faction pursued its own distinct policy toward the Black Movement and that that policy was based on divergent ideologies and views on Cuban security.

The Guevarist position was reinforced in the March 1962 "sectarian crisis" when "Stalinist" Communist Party members (recently appointed by pro-Moscow faction leader Aníbal Escalante) were purged from office and replaced with "revolutionaries" from Castro and Guevara's camp. During the crisis Castro also accused Escalante of opposing the insurrectional platform put forth in the "Second Declaration of Havana."[11] Ironically, two weeks later, the Soviet news organ *Pravda* finally acknowledged Cuba as a socialist country and relations between the Soviets and the Cuban regime began to be strengthened.

As pointed out in the previous discussion on ideological differences, in the aftermath of the 1962 Missile Crisis, pro-USSR Communist Party members again lost credibility in the regime with the result that the Guevarists enjoyed another brief rise in their ability to set the security agenda and internal policies. Nonetheless, within two years, Guevara himself grew frustrated with the slowness of Cuba's industrialization under his own direction. By 1964, it was apparent that his 1961 four-year plan of industrialization had been a failure.[12] More and more he realized that the stability of the regime depended on dynamics and forces on the international plane, forces over which Cuba could exert very little control without risking certain retaliation or isolation and internal collapse.[13]

But the failure of Guevara's industrialization plan had broader security ramifications which would impede Cuba's march toward a socialist state. Guevara conceded:

> There couldn't be a revolution without industrialization, and there couldn't be industries without markets. To obtain markets the revolution would have to continue in Latin America, in which case the United States would call the USSR to task [since, in exchange for U.S. nonintervention in Cuba after the Missile Crisis, the Soviets assured Washington that Cuba would not expand its political influence in the hemisphere], and if Cuba did not listen to the USSR, the latter would end her commitment to the Cuban socialist regime. That, of course, would mean the end of the Revolution. Everyone knew that only the immense military strength of Russia could balance that of the United States and prevent a devastating attack from the north.[14]

It appeared that Guevara could not see a way out of this inevitable slide into adopting Soviet prescriptions for security, meaning that Cuba would have to cease its support for revolution in the hemisphere. He nonetheless railed against the pro-Moscow path, which he saw would perpetuate Cuba's weak economy and its indefinite dependence on the Soviets for protection. "The revolution," Che told a friend, "was not fought for that."[15]

Castro seemed caught in the middle between his instinctual agreement with Guevara and his pragmatic view of the immediate security crisis in Cuba. "For Castro himself," writes Moore, "the dependent relationship posed the problem of how Cuba could enjoy Soviet military protection and economic aid without becoming a mere Caribbean satellite of the USSR."[16] A compromise between the two camps was apparently reached around mid-decade, most likely brokered by Castro who was once again playing the role of accommodationist bridging the two "extremes": The traditional Communist Party's approach to security would be used in policies toward the U.S. Movement, but the Guevarist approach would be intensified in the Third World.

This two-tiered policy vis-á-vis insurrectional support allowed for a revolutionary stance toward those countries from which the Cubans did not fear retaliation and a more cautious approach toward the United States and its revolutionary movement. Perhaps Moscow was putting less pressure on the Cubans at that time with regard to support for Third World insurrection, allowing the revolutionary elements to operate with little interference from the Kremlin. In any event, Cuba began a campaign in Latin America in 1964 to garner support for the Cuban Revolution and create "two, three, many Vietnams."

Therefore, in the early months of 1965, Guevara's approach to security had been effectively defeated by the traditional Communist Party faction with regard to the U.S. Movement. Before Che could attempt to push for a more militant policy toward the U.S. Black Movement, he disappeared. In addition, those closest to him were either demoted, transferred to the provinces or sent to Africa on international missions.

These crucial years of a turning toward conservative policies posed many challenges for the Castro government; with respect to the U.S. Movement, however, the official rhetoric did not change. As a result, U.S. Black Nationalists would not learn of the change in policy and priorities until they came face to face with revisionism while in exile. Around that time, Williams speculated that a deal had actually been struck between elements within Cuban intelligence and the CIA to silence him and other Black exiles and to halt Cuban support for revolution within the United States in general in exchange for a U.S. pledge of nonintervention in Cuba.[17]

The reason why the Cuban leadership entrusted its intelligence and security apparatus, the DGI, with relations toward the U.S. Black Movement deserves some explanation. The DGI, commonly referred to as the G-2, is part of the Ministry of Interior (MININT), which "was one of the most strategically important agencies in Cuba. Not only was it responsible for the police, exit permits, and other functions, but MININT had the heavy duty of fighting the enemies of the revolution."[18] Although a cultural institution was a more appropriate liaison in the decade of the 1970s and beyond as the nature of relations among the regime, U.S. Blacks, and Afro-Cubans became less political and more focused on cultural and educational linkages, this was not the case during the politically volatile decade of the 1960s. Both the Cubans and the U.S. Black leadership perceived the other as a potential political ally, while simultaneously the CIA interpreted any contact between the U.S.

militants and the island as politically subversive and potentially danger-ous to U.S. national security.

Indeed, given the confrontational tone of relations between Cuba and Washington, security issues were at the forefront in any dealings with U.S. nationals. Finally, regarding the high-risk activity of air piracy, or hijack-ing, the DGI was paramount in monitoring every stage of this activity, from a rogue plane entering Cuban airspace to interrogation of individuals arriving in this way, in order to prevent CIA infiltration or attack.

Given the political climate in 1965—a tougher official stance toward the Cuban regime by President Johnson had made efforts of rapproche-ment uncertain, the U.S. invasion of the Dominican Republic, and the escalation of the wars in Vietnam and the Congo—the dominant pro-Moscow camp realized that it had to be even more careful. Cuban national security concerns were most acute during the Black Nationalist stage of the U.S. struggle not only because of these factors but also because of the more radicalized nature of the U.S. Movement.

At the same time, the pro-Soviet-dominated regime had less of a desire to act aggressively. In their view, the key to weakening both U.S. external interventionist patterns and internal stability lay in the Vietnam conflict. The regime saw the role of the Black militants as one of support for the larger Anti-War Movement with the goal of weakening U.S. hegemony from within and outside in order to ensure Cuba's survival. "Fighting in the rear" was their hope for a diversion of U.S. aggression away from the island.[19]

Rojo states that as late as 1967, Castro was nonetheless in complete agreement with the organization of a guerrilla insurrection in Bolivia. A success in Bolivia might reinvigorate the hemispheric struggle, affording Cuba more natural allies and a position of leadership in the future, whereas currently it was sinking into a submissive, satellite position. Both Guevara and Castro also realized the important security ramifications of having a socialist neighbor closer than the Urals.[20] But, Fidel drew much criticism over this issue. He was accused of not being a "true revolutionary" by pro-Moscow officials, who felt that his support for external insurrection and his acting on "sentimental impulse" with groups and individuals such as the U.S. Blacks came at the cost of adhering to strict ideological tenets.[21]

After the failure of the Bolivian experiment resulting in Che's death in 1967, Castro chose a client-patron relationship with the Soviets as the only way he and the traditional Party members could see to preserve the

Revolution, uphold a degree of national sovereignty, and maintain power. Increasingly, his hands were tied by the shrinking political space to maneuver within the East-West world-security paradigm and by the suppression of alternative perspectives to Soviet dictates.

THE U.S. THREAT TO CUBAN SECURITY

U.S. intervention designed to destabilize the new regime was Cuba's primary security concern throughout the decade. Beginning in 1960, relations between the two countries deteriorated quickly. In August, the United States took the first steps to garner hemispheric support for an impending invasion of the island by presenting a White Paper to the OAS in which it condemned the Cubans as guerrillas and Communist agents bent on spreading violent revolution throughout the hemisphere.[22] On 19 October 1960 the United States declared a trade embargo against Cuba and recalled its ambassadors three days later. Soon after, Havana learned of Cuban exiles being organized by the CIA to launch an attack against the island from Guatemala, Nicaragua and Honduras.[23] Diplomatic relations were broken off between the two countries on 3 January 1961; not long after, Cuba prepared for an inevitable attack as Soviet military hardware was shipped to the island for the defense of the Revolution.

The Castro regime had hopes that the new U.S. president, John Kennedy, would seek a softer line than had his predecessor. These hopes were dashed when Kennedy delivered a speech on the infiltration of Communist influences into the hemispheric insurrectional movements. A recently released and highly self-critical report written by CIA Inspector General Lyman Kirkpatrick divulges that Kennedy was actually in a poor position to reverse the plans for invasion, which had been in the works since well before the new president assumed office. The report states that the CIA "had failed to advise the President [who had taken office just three months prior to the attack], at an appropriate time, that success had become dubious and to recommend that the operation be therefore canceled and that the problem of unseating Castro be restudied."[24]

Coinciding with Kennedy's aggressive speech was an increased activity of saboteurs and terrorist bombs in Cuban cities, and the concentration of counterrevolutionary forces in the Sierra del Escambray.[25] The entire island was mobilized for war on all fronts, and tensions were wearing thin. Finally, on 15 April, through a CIA-led effort, Cuban airfields were bombed; two days later, "an unruly, ill-trained, and crudely supported invasion force"[26] of 1,511 landed on Cuban shores. Within three days of fighting, the counterrevolutionaries had been defeated, and Cuban defiance of U.S. imperialism took on legendary proportions.

The fundamental reason for this disaster was not Kennedy's halting of further air strikes, as was widely believed, but rather the CIA's admitted incompetence. The agency was unwilling to call off the invasion, which resulted in the deaths of nearly every man sent to capture the island, because, in their words, "cancellation would have been embarrassing."[27] In retrospect, the CIA confessed that better planning and scrutiny on their part prior to the invasion,

> would also have raised the question of why the United States should contemplate pitting 1,500 soldiers, however well trained and armed, against an enemy vastly superior in number and armament on a terrain which offered nothing but vague hope of significant local support. It might also have suggested that the agency's responsibility in the operation should be drastically revised and would certainly have revealed that there was no real plan for the post-invasion period, whether for success or failure. . . .[28]

THE CUBAN MISSILE CRISIS

The international event that perhaps best demonstrates the quick ascension of the traditional Communist Party approach to security followed by its abrupt loss of credibility, was the Missile Crisis. In the summer of 1962, the Kremlin and Havana had secretly agreed to arm Cuba with nuclear weapons.[29] The first shipment of nuclear missiles arrived in Havana in early September. This, along with thousands of Soviet military forces and other major weaponry, made Cuba almost overnight the most heavily armed Third World country. The maintenance of this force would serve the several purposes of altering the balance of power, deterring U.S. aggression against the Soviet Union, protecting Cuba from another U.S. attack and affording the Soviets a nuclear and military presence in the western hemisphere previously unimagined.

But on 22 October, Washington publicly exposed this buildup; six days later, faced with mounting threats from the United States and the threat of an East-West nuclear confrontation, the Soviets capitulated and withdrew the forty-two missiles without consulting Castro.[30] When Castro received word from the press—not even from the Soviets themselves—of the withdrawal, he was obviously humiliated and infuriated. Consequently, Soviet advisors and those within the Cuban Communist Party wedded to Soviet dictates became much less conspicuous in setting policy over the following months.

Although Cuba lost its nuclear warheads and bombers, it was left with the most sophisticated defense system in the Third World. This system and Kennedy's nonintervention pledge, which had been negotiated by the USSR, provided Castro with a certain level of security three years into the nascent regime. Still, CIA sabotage and foreign-inspired assassination attempts persisted.[31]

Cuban security witnessed a watershed year in 1965 as the Guevarists were effectively purged from power, the Moscow-oriented officials consolidated their influence within the regime, and the U.S. rhetoric toward the island turned more hostile. Aside from feeble efforts to continue secret, bilateral negotiations, President Johnson turned up the pressure on the Cuban regime, agreeing to numerous assassination attempts on Cuban leaders, repeated violation of Cuban airspace, and utilization of the Guantánamo base for harassing the population and illegal activities.[32] In hemispheric relations, Johnson won even stauncher condemnations of Cuba from the OAS that same year, a move that further isolated the regime and threatened both its internal and external security.

Relations with the Nixon administration showed little improvement. Despite an extensive study conducted by the CIA between 1969 and 1970 refuting the rumor that the Black Panthers were being covertly supported by Cuba,[33] the new president opened twenty FBI intelligence posts in foreign countries in an attempt to discover these elusive international links to the domestic movement. The CIA report affirmed that the roots of the Black and Peace movements were to be found in U.S. racial injustice and the Vietnam War, not foreign agitation. Fearing that the CIA was not sufficiently vigilant in its investigations, Nixon and Secretary of State Kissinger essentially mandated the FBI to assume CIA responsibilities. In reality, by the late 1960s, the traditional Communist Party influence had so effectively changed the nature of Cuban relations with the U.S. Movement to a conservative position that any acts beyond lip service to international solidarity were negligible.

ISSUES OF PERSONAL SAFETY AND THE CUBAN SECURITY POLICY

Every U.S. Black leader was faced with threats to personal security throughout both stages of the 1960s Movement. The FBI began its surveillance of the SCLC, King and the Nation of Islam in the late 1950s and of SNCC in 1960.[34] Efforts were stepped up in the first part of the 1960s against King, Malcolm X, Stokely Carmichael, and the Black Panther Party and escalated throughout the decade.[35] As these Black leaders' criticism of U.S. racism and imperialism grew, so did the surveillance as well as harassment and death threats against them. The threat of government-sponsored harassment and even murder intensified after the controversial assassinations of Malcolm X in 1965 and King in 1968.

On 25 August 1967 the FBI officially launched a massive counterintelligence program (COINTELPRO) in an all-out effort to divide, infiltrate, and essentially break the Black Nationalist movement. FBI Director Hoover described the Panthers, who were the main focus of the government assault, as posing "the greatest threat to the internal security of the country."[36] The COINTELPRO operation included spying, wiretapping, burglaries, and infiltration in order to create disruption and paranoia within select radical groups. In addition to the Black Panther Party, these targeted organizations included potential Arab terrorist groups, radical ethnic and student organizations and suspected Soviet espionage groups such as U.S. Marxist parties.[37]

Compounding the official harassment was ongoing racial violence wielded by private hate groups and individuals. King's home was firebombed in 1956; Black churches were burned throughout the South; lynchings were commonplace; Blacks were fired from their jobs, evicted from their homes, and in many other ways terrorized in order that they would not take up the cause of desegregation, let alone pick up a gun. In desperate reaction to this violence and repression, the cry of "Burn baby burn" rose out of Watts in 1965, and by 1967 cities throughout the country were ablaze with Black retaliatory violence.

EXILE IN CUBA

In response also to this climate of harassment, violence, and continuing threats to personal security, many Black fighters sought exile in Cuba, at times at the invitation of Castro himself. The reality of desperate exiles seeking refuge in an allegedly revolutionary state threw into sharp relief the debate between the Guevarist and traditional Communist Party camps over the best strategy for national security. The limits to Cuban solidarity were thus tested throughout the decade and beyond by such leaders as Williams, the Panther Party's Cleaver, Newton, and Assata Shakur, and countless other Black militants of all persuasions. In order to illustrate the erratic shifts in policy toward the U.S Black Movement springing from the conflict between the two camps over national security and ideology, it is important to review the two most significant exile experiences in the decade of the 1960s, those of Robert Williams and Eldridge Cleaver.

Robert Williams

A former NAACP leader yet longtime advocate of armed self-defense among Blacks, Williams had been one of the first travelers to Cuba with the Fair Play for Cuba Committee, an organization established in the spring of 1960 to support the Castro-led Revolution and to assist travel between the two countries.[38] An outspoken opponent of the Bay of Pigs invasion and other hostility against Cuba, he soon became a target of FBI aggression. In August 1961, the Bureau attempted to crush Williams' burgeoning self-defense committees which had been amassing arms in North Carolina.

In October, Williams fled to Cuba through Tijuana, Mexico, after a violent clash between White racists, the police and the Freedom Riders, a direct action group organized by CORE. This clash led to an FBI warrant for Williams' arrest on what were most likely fabricated charges of kidnapping and interstate flight. At the personal invitation of Castro, Williams was able to enter Cuba.[39] This escape led to the first highly publicized relationship between a U.S. Black leader and the Cuban government in this era.

Within a short time in Cuba, Williams established links to bring more Black activists to the island via Canada, began broadcasting the pro-Castro radio show "Radio Free Dixie" calling for a repeat of the Sierra Maestra insurrection to be mounted in the U.S. South, and spoke at public rallies with Castro as well as at private receptions for all African delegations to the island.[40] Initially, the political climate was favorable to Williams' brand of militancy, since the Guevarist approach to security was still considered to be a viable option. At that time, many within the regime, including Castro, were almost literally thumbing their noses at the United States and had not realized their "proper place" within the mounting East-West conflict.

Once in exile, Williams was anxious to discuss the militant tactics outlined in his book *Theory of Urban Warfare*. In it, he had asserted that the vanguard Black revolutionaries would carry out an urban guerrilla campaign. However, it was this subject that would soon lead him to discover the disparity between Cuban revolutionary rhetoric and the actions many were willing to take on behalf of U.S. Black liberation; it was on this issue that he first clashed with traditional Communist Party forces over Cuban security.[41]

Within the first years of his exile, members of the increasingly pro-Soviet DGI and the Communist Party were becoming unwilling to entertain a public discussion of his tactics, particularly given the fragility of U.S.-Cuban relations in 1962. When the leadership continually sought to discourage his plans for a guerrilla "foco" in the U.S. South, he grew frustrated. With hindsight, it seems Williams would have fared better with the Cubans had he been a peasant in the Andes rather than an urban dweller from the United States. To the pro-Moscow Cubans, the correct approach for the Third World was dangerous to attempt in the First World.

His radio program was another point of contention with the traditional Communists. According to Amuchastegui, the extremist views that Williams broadcasted over Radio Havana could not be tolerated, strictly for security purposes.[42] His requests for accusatory speech leveled at the United States from the Cuban government were denied. The pro-Soviets also tried to dissuade Williams from drawing international attention to racism in the United States.[43] They saw this as both dangerous to Cuban security and divisive in terms of long-term solidarity with the U.S. working class.

Castro, at that time very much in agreement with the Guevarist approach to national security, went against pro-Moscow advice and granted Williams additional assistance in broadcasting his program.[44] Fidel attempted to help him on a number of occasions when the Communist stalwarts were sabotaging his broadcasts or disrupting the printing of his newspaper, *The Crusader*.[45] Castro also offered assistance in publishing Williams' book *Negroes With Guns*.

But as the decade progressed, the pro-Soviets erected obstacles between Williams and his sympathizers within the upper echelon of the regime. One CPUSA advisor working in Cuban radio at the time informed

Williams, "Just remember, Fidel is way up there at the top and you are way down here at the bottom; and there are a lot of us in between who can mess you up very badly without him ever hearing about it."[46] The "Bourgeois Communists" apparently worked in conjunction with the CPUSA to smear Williams and otherwise diminish his reach and influence throughout North America.

By early 1965 as the Moscow-oriented elements consolidated their authority, sabotage of Williams' projects worsened.[47] Many within the regime grew more and more opposed to Williams' anti-Washington inflammatory rhetoric, concluding that it was jeopardizing Cuban security.[48] Williams came to suspect that certain members of the DGI and the government were actually working with U.S. intelligence to get him thrown out of Cuba and returned to the United States to face the criminal charges against him. This would remove a major point of contention, so the traditional Communists reasoned, in U.S.-Cuban relations and could potentially be a move toward a guarantee of Cuban territorial integrity. The mounting efforts against Williams led to his grudging conclusion that the revolutionary dynamic that he had fallen in love with at the dawn of the decade had been crippled by party elitism and the Cold War orientation toward national security. With this disappointing conclusion, he began to make plans to leave Cuba for China, a place for which he still harbored revolutionary hopes and from which he expected support for U.S. Black liberation.[49]

Three months before Williams' departure, Guevara all but admitted defeat of his security and ideological positions in a secret meeting with Williams. Guevara vehemently stated his total disagreement with the direction in which the Communist Party was steering the country as well as its conservative approach to the U.S. Black Movement.[50] Within weeks of that meeting, the Guevarists would be permanently sealed from power, thus determining Williams' fate in Cuba. The following year, Williams was not invited to the first Tricontinental Conference held in Havana and organized by the Party for African, Asian and American "revolutionaries." He therefore concluded that "as long as Cuba's leaders believed the only way for their nation to survive was to avoid seriously irritating Washington, there was no hope of their giving anything but hollow words of support to the Black Liberation Movement in America."[51] As things went from bad to worse, Williams came to blows with the Cuban security forces. According to Cleaver, who spoke at length with Williams later in Tanzania, the

"Bourgeois Communists" closed down his radio program, forbade printing any more newsletters and were forcibly moving him out of his apartment. Shots were allegedly exchanged in anger between Williams and the police.[52]

After learning of these incidents and of Williams' plans to leave, Castro sent three loyal officials to plead with Williams to reconsider. They said they realized the government had lost some of its pure revolutionary ideals but that Fidel needed people like Williams to stay and fight for the soul of the Revolution. In the opinion of these men, the most serious problem within the leadership at the time was that Castro was being isolated and misinformed by the pro-Moscow advisors around him.[53] Williams, however, knew his battle lay elsewhere, in the liberation of his own people.

He had also lost faith in Castro's ability to effect radical change, particularly after the purging of Guevara's influence from the regime. Although Williams felt Castro's heart lay with the armed struggle for liberation, he saw that what the man was willing to do as an individual and what he could do as head of state were radically different. Williams now understood that Cuba's degradation into a bureaucratized state necessitated the isolation of its revolutionaries, like Che and Fidel, since the existence of charismatic personalities posed a continual threat to the bureaucrat.[54] For Castro to survive as the leader of Cuba, he had to be either convinced of, or forced to accept, the traditional Communist Party faction security policies.

Williams left for China on 17 July 1966. He soon wrote a letter to Castro that was allegedly blocked from reaching him by Williams' enemies within Cuba; he therefore sent it as an open letter through press channels. In it, he thanked Fidel for the Cubans' hospitality and pledged his support for the Revolution, but said that he wanted to draw Castro's attention to certain revisionist leaders within the regime who posed a threat to the very survival of the Cuban Revolution. He accused Major Manuel Piñeiro Losado (head of the DGI), René Vallejo (Castro's personal aide and physician) and Osmany Cienfuegos (Minister of Construction) of being thieves or worse.[55] This letter was Williams' final attempt to reach a leader he deemed isolated and misled from the revolutionary path, one who was allowing conservative policies to be implemented toward the U.S. Black Movement because of misguided security concerns.

Eldridge Cleaver

Security policy at the time of Cleaver's exile was for the most part solidly under the control of traditional Communist dictates. Still, given domestic security ramifications, the "Bourgeois Communists" could not afford to give up the revolutionary facade perpetuated by bold phrases of official international solidarity and support for insurrection. Consequently, asylum was granted to the Black Panther leader in late 1968.[56]

Cleaver was under ongoing assault from the COINTELPRO effort to eliminate the Black Panthers and, after an April 6 shoot-out with Oakland police, secretly requested asylum through a Cuban representative to the United Nations in New York. Cleaver asked for special assurance from Castro himself that he would be received as a fugitive under Cleaver's own conditions.[57] After much debate on the issue of risking retaliation from the United States, the Cuban regime acceded to his request.[58]

Cleaver received word through the Cuban mission in New York that Fidel had accepted his conditions and that he would be granted asylum under no pressure to leave; he was assured of "safe passage, security, and help." In addition, Castro indicated that Cleaver would be in charge of organizing the start-up of a military training facility on an abandoned farm outside of Havana which the Cubans had promised the Black Panther Party some time earlier. After an arduous escape, Cleaver arrived in Havana on Christmas morning 1968.[59]

The Panther leader was in complete agreement with the Cubans that his exile be kept as discreet as possible. He understood that if the U.S. government found out that Cuba was harboring militant fugitives, it would have a good excuse to accuse the regime of meddling in U.S. internal affairs and a justification for overt or covert aggression against the island. This was a deep concern for both Cleaver and the Cubans, and they discussed it at length in the planning stages of Cleaver's flight into exile.[60]

While in Havana, his stay was supervised by Major Piñeiro. Cleaver also had a security official, Mr. Silva, assigned to check up on him daily and monitor his behavior for the government. Cleaver's relationship with Castro himself remained formal, but he had much back-and-forth discussion through the third parties of Piñeiro, Silva, two officials from the Communist Party, and Mr. Arbesu, a liaison between the Cuban government and the Palestinian movement in Lebanon[61] who was later appointed head of the Cuban Interest Section in the United States.

Aside from the ongoing delays in opening the training facility, another major point of contention between Cleaver—along with other exiled Black militants in general—and the Cuban government was the issue of the treatment of hijackers. "Air piracy," as it was officially branded, had become a chronic security threat for the Cuban leadership throughout the late 1960s and 1970s. Amuchastegui disputes Moore's assertion that the Cuban government was "delighted" over the incessant operations and rather claims that, from the onset, the Cubans were trying to come to an agreement with the United States on this issue.[62] In 1973, Havana and Washington at last reached a bilateral anti-hijacking agreement, the first major accord between the two governments since 1959.

The Cubans did of course use the incidents to embarrass the U.S. government internationally. Their exploitation of these events was much like the media attention given by the U.S. press when exiles would make their escape *from* Cuba. Nonetheless, risks were high since the Cubans did not know if these planes were on a mission to attack the island (à la Bay of Pigs), if they carried CIA or FBI spies posing as U.S. dissidents, or if they brought genuine fighters fleeing the United States for political reasons.

There was some justifiable confusion and frustration for hijackers once they landed in Cuba, thinking they had reached freedom, only to be greeted by security forces and jailed until a determination could be made as to their identity and motives. The Cubans maintain, however, that this was a standard and necessary procedure. They insist that the idea of Cuba as a welcoming haven for oppressed Black revolutionaries was correct to a point but that this welcome was never intended for those who resorted to air piracy as their means of transport.[63]

Cleaver conceded that some security procedures were necessary in order to guard against counterrevolutionary forces, but what most upset him were the stories of inhumane acts against Cubans witnessed by the U.S. Blacks while in prison. To him, such actions were unworthy of a "proletarian dictatorship."[64] He first learned of this maltreatment from former New York Panthers who had been temporarily incarcerated after hijacking planes to Cuba.[65] They were routinely sent to the "fearsome work camp," as they described it to Cleaver, of Lucarenia in Oriente Province. Cleaver arranged for one of the hijackers, who had been released, to return to Lucarenia in order to give the other Panthers Cleaver's address in Havana and encourage them to run away.[66] Some, like Byron Booth, made a couple of unsuccessful attempts before finally escaping to Havana.[67]

Cleaver confronted the Cubans about the conditions of both imprisoned Cubans and the internment process of U.S. hijackers. The government in turn accused Cleaver of meddling in their internal affairs. As word spread and the number of Cleaver's roommates swelled, suspicion grew among Cuban security forces. When Silva admonished him with allegations of jeopardizing internal security, Cleaver proclaimed that he had now assembled enough Black Panthers (all under his own roof) to begin training the first class at the farm facility outside Havana. With this, he thought, the Cubans could no longer make excuses for the constant delays in beginning the training that had frustrated him for months.[68]

Silva finally admitted that the government could not abide by their agreement to train the Black Panthers for two reasons. First, they had concluded that the Black protest movement had become so infiltrated by FBI and CIA agents that they did not know whom they could and could not trust. Training and arming the U.S. Movement in Cuba would pose a great threat to internal security by opening the possibility of mistakenly arming undercover counterrevolutionaries; it would also threaten Cuba's national security should U.S. intelligence learn of their assistance and thus feel justified to attack. The second reason the Cubans gave was that, since Guevara's death, the policy of active assistance to liberation struggles had been discontinued. At the time, Cleaver took the Cubans at their word and believed that, in first promising the training facility to the Panthers, they had been sincere.[69]

What seems most likely is that the Cuban representatives to the United Nations maintained a Guevarist approach to the U.S. Movement longer than the majority of the leadership on the island did. Therefore, these representatives were still promising revolutionary support as late as 1967 or 1968 to Black militants in the United States, even though this practice had been deemed insupportable by the bulk of the regime in Havana by mid-decade.

Indeed, Amuchastegui, who was the first Cuban official to meet with Cleaver apart from intelligence channels when he first arrived, claims that throughout Cleaver's stay in Havana the government attempted to redirect his revolutionary thinking away from armed struggle, since the conditions did not exist within the United States for it even to be considered. The Cubans also understood that public statements emanating from Havana from a top Black Panther leader could have disastrous effects on the safety of the country. In the late 1960s, according to Amuchastegui, they were not willing to risk almost certain retaliation for *any* leader.[70]

The final straw came when a Reuters reporter learned that Cleaver was in Havana and confronted him at his apartment. Both Cleaver and the Cubans knew that the U.S. government might use the discovery as an excuse to retaliate. But Cleaver was concerned for his own safety on two sides: Not only was he a fugitive from U.S. law, but given his constant conflicts with the Cuban government and increasing disillusionment in the face of what he saw as reactionary features in the regime and within Cuban society itself, he no longer felt safe in the care of his Cuban hosts.[71]

The Cubans, with Cleaver's consent, arranged for him to leave the island temporarily in May 1969 and seek refuge in a Palestinian camp in Lebanon, to which he would be escorted by Arbesu. When he arrived in Algeria en route to Lebanon, however, Cleaver encountered friends working with the Algerian government who persuaded him to stay and establish the Black Panther Party international headquarters in Algiers, despite Cuban warnings that he was not welcome by the Algerian government.[72]

Author Michael Newton suggests a slightly different reason for Cleaver's departure. He proposes that Fidel actually told the Panthers that they needed to find another international base of operations. This was done, asserts Newton, because the Castro regime was at that time seeking improved relations with the U.S. government and was growing embarrassed by the mounting number of hijackings to Cuba carried out by Black militants.[73] While Newton's analysis of the regime is correct, Cleaver maintains that Castro never told him to leave; rather, he decided to go mainly because of his own concern for personal security as well as his disillusionment with the revisionist policies of the regime in the late 1960s.[74]

NOTES

1. Rojo, 94.
2. Amuchastegui, interview.
3. Cohen, 314.
4. Amuchastegui, interview.
5. Ibid.
6. Rojo, 85.
7. Ibid., 86.
8. Ibid., 111.
9. Amuchastegui, interview.
10. Moore, 120.

11. Fidel Castro, "Algunos problemas de los métodos y formas de trabajo de las ORI" [Some Problems of the Methods and Functioning of the ORI], *Obra Revolucionaria* [Havana] 10 (1962): 7–32.

12. Rojo, 165.

13. Ibid., 136.

14. Ibid., 166.

15. Quoted in Ibid.

16. Moore, 4.

17. Cohen, 302.

18. Llovio-Menéndez, 119–20.

19. Amuchastegui, interview.

20. Rojo, 191.

21. Cohen, 233.

22. Sobel, 17.

23. Hugh Thomas, *Cuba, or the Pursuit of Freedom* (London: Eyre & Spottiswoode, 1971), 1300–11.

24. Central Intelligence Agency, *The Inspector General's Survey of the Cuban Operation* (Washington, D.C.: The National Security Archive, 1961), sec. 31. b. Document available at the archive's web site: http://www.seas.gwu.edu/nsarchive; and Tim Weiner, "C.I.A. Bares Own Bungling in '61 Report on Bay of Pigs," *New York Times*, 22 February 1998, 1, 6.

25. Rojo, 96.

26. Weiner, 6.

27. CIA, sec. 37.

28. Ibid., sec. 33.

29. Nikita Krushchev, *Krushchev Remembers*, ed. Edward Crankshaw (Boston: Little, Brown & Co., 1970), 493.

30. Rojo, 133.

31. Moore, 137.

32. Semidei, 152–56.

33. Seymour M. Hersh, "Alien-Radical Tie Disputed by C.I.A.," *New York Times*, 25 May 1973, 1.

34. Ward Churchill, *The COINTELPRO Papers* (Boston: South End Press, 1990), 95–96, 102–3.

35. Ibid., 105–230.

36. JoNina M. Abron, "The Legacy of the Black Panther Party," *The Black Scholar* (November-December 1968): 33.

37. Hersh, 1.

38. Moore, 60.

39. Cohen, 225.

40. Moore, 121–22.

41. Cohen, 225.

42. Amuchastegui, interview.
43. Ibid.; and Cohen, 208.
44. Cohen, 210.
45. Ibid., 223–25.
46. Quoted in Ibid., 302. The advisor is not identified.
47. Ibid., 209.
48. Cleaver, interview; and Amuchastegui, interview.
49. Cohen, 302.
50. Ibid., 292.
51. Ibid., 314.
52. Cleaver, interview.
53. Cohen, 313.
54. Ibid., 315.
55. Ibid., 320.
56. Amuchastegui, interview.
57. Cleaver, interview.
58. Amuchastegui, interview.
59. Cleaver, interview.
60. Ibid.
61. Ibid.
62. Amuchastegui, interview.
63. Ibid.
64. Cleaver, interview.
65. See William Lee Brent, *Long Time Gone* (New York: Random House, 1996); and John Clytus with Jane Rieker, *Black Man in Red Cuba* (Coral Gables, Fla.: University of Miami Press, 1970).
66. Cleaver, interview.
67. Ibid.
68. Ibid.
69. Ibid.
70. Amuchastegui, interview.
71. Cleaver, interview.
72. Ibid.
73. Michael Newton, *Bitter Grain: Huey Newton and the Black Panther Party* (Los Angeles: Holloway House Publishing Company, 1991), 117–18.
74. Cleaver, interview.

EXPECTATIONS

T he U.S. political climate of the mid-1960s was changing drastically: The Civil Rights Movement splintered and, in its place, Black Nationalism and militancy surged into the limelight; U.S. intervention was on the rise in the Caribbean; the war in Vietnam escalated. But despite the emerging opportunities for "revolutionary" Cuba to deepen relations significantly with the radicalizing U.S. Left, Cuban expectations of Black leadership changed little from the early part of the decade and, as with other issues, depended primarily on which Cuban faction was gaining power, regardless of the nature of the U.S. leadership itself.

CUBAN EXPECTATIONS

Merging the African American Struggle with the Peace Movement

Both the Guevarist camp and the traditional Communist Party faction expected and encouraged the U.S. militants to link their struggle with the growing Anti-War Movement in the United States. Their reasoning was that this would serve, first, to weaken U.S. interventionist foreign policy so that, in the short term, Washington would be preoccupied with growing domestic unrest and less likely to embark on a large-scale attack against Cuba; and second, that in the longer run, North Vietnam might triumph as a Communist revolutionary state and Cuba would gain a new ally. In time, the Cubans hoped a strong coalition of the U.S. Left in solidarity with the Cuban regime would force Washington's hand, compelling it to cease its interventionist policies, to the ultimate benefit of Cuba and other fledgling socialist states. These expectations and objectives were shared by both Cuban camps.

Cuban President Osvaldo Dórticos Torrado revealed this thinking, represented by many within the regime, in a statement in 1967. The expanding U.S. Black revolt, he declared, demonstrated the "internal contradictions which . . . inhibit the combat capacity of [U.S.] imperialism to combat revolutionary movements by its having to be concerned over its own domestic front and which reveal . . . its incapacity to guarantee . . . the survival of national oligarchies."[1] Taking a further step, the Cubans urged U.S. Blacks to make the most of these "internal contradictions," by laying aside differences with, or misgivings about, White workers and liberals and melding their common interests into a unified struggle.

The Guevarist camp, as mentioned previously, did not rule out the possibility of a Black-led U.S. revolution; in fact, this was their highest aspiration for the U.S. Movement. But they knew that a two-pronged approach had to take place, namely, the uniting of Black factions around the use of revolutionary violence as well as a massive stirring of class consciousness among U.S. workers in support of the most radical Left, the U.S. Blacks. Since the Guevarists held that Cuban security would be best ensured by a promotion of revolution worldwide, and did not make distinctions based on the dominant Cold War balance-of-power paradigm, a successful U.S. insurrection, though remote, would be the ultimate safeguard of Cuban security.

The two factions repeatedly urged the Black leaders who visited the island to join the broader Peace Movement. The Black leaders, in turn, had different responses to this expectation. Those who fulfilled the expectation of attempting to merge the struggle with the Anti-War Movement included King, Cleaver and the Black Panther Party, and Davis.

King's coalition-building philosophy was lauded by both camps, and many within the pro-Soviet camp viewed him as the leader most able to merge the Black struggle with the Anti-War Movement. This hope began to be fulfilled a year before King's assassination, as he started to express sympathy with the Vietnamese people and denounce the U.S. war effort publicly. To the dominant Cuban leadership at the time, his death in 1968 was a severe setback to bringing the more moderate sectors of the Black Movement into the large Anti-War lobby.

Around the same time, the Black Panthers to some extent fulfilled this expectation, albeit drawing their support from more radical sectors than had the civil rights leader. They actively sought alliances with such groups as the SDS and, later, the Weather Underground, both predominantly White. White sympathizers were entrusted with important, high-risk tasks, including acting as messengers to jailed Panther Party members, harboring Cleaver in Berkeley, California, and in Canada while he was a fugitive, and then facilitating his successful escape to Cuba. The Panthers propagated solidarity with, and victory for, the Vietcong, called for an end to U.S. imperialism, and believed in a multiracial, united front that could ignite the insurrection.[2]

Davis, too, fulfilled the expectation of both Cuban camps. Her early dedication to an interracial confederation to advance the struggle for civil rights continued into her Communist years. Since she believed that Black liberation would only come about through the complete overthrow of the U.S. capitalist system, she felt that Blacks, given their small numbers, needed the active support of Marxists everywhere, first and foremost at home. Therefore, Davis converged with the Cubans on this important expectation.

Other leaders, however, who bore Pan-Africanist or separatist leanings, balked at the Cubans' suggestion to join the largely White Peace Movement. To these leaders, this expectation was so great a source of frustration and disillusionment that it led to charges of racism and betrayal against the Cuban government. Those who failed to live up to this expectation included Williams, Malcolm X and Carmichael. Williams' ongoing contacts with White American leftists of every stripe served to reinforce his distrust of their dedication to Black liberation. The mounting struggle in Vietnam throughout the mid-decade was only of peripheral concern to Williams; he maintained as his primary goal a Black liberation led by predominantly Black organizations. Therefore, he failed to support the Cubans' hope of merging with the Anti-War lobby, to the frustration of the traditional Communists and, to a lesser degree, the Guevarists.

Malcolm X was assassinated in 1965 and so did not have the chance to demonstrate concretely to the Cubans his emerging stance on the war in Vietnam. If the Cubans judged him on his earlier convictions—racial separation and refusing to take part in the integrationist Civil Rights struggle or to work with Whites for any reason—neither the Guevarists nor the pro-Soviets would have much reason to expect that he would be the leader to merge the struggles. His turn to a guarded yet conciliatory stance toward some Whites, along with his growing internationalist perspective and solidarity with the people of Vietnam, pointed out the direction in which Malcolm was heading in the final year of his life. Despite this shift, it remains unlikely that, given his strong dedication to his race and his religion, he would have satisfactorily fulfilled the Cubans' expectation of advocating a full merging of the two movements.

Carmichael vehemently disagreed with the Cubans on this matter. He frequently reminded audiences of the history of failed interracial coalitions and betrayals at important moments and was convinced that White liberals would not fight to the end to achieve the objectives of the Black struggle. He, and other nationalists with a similar ideology, initially felt betrayed by the Cubans for even suggesting such a union, much less continually pressing the issue with Black leaders in exile. This is the expectation around which relations between the Cubans and Carmichael would break down in 1967.

Solidarity

Both factions of the Cuban leadership desired solidarity with sympathizers within the United States. Since risk of a U.S. invasion was the primary security concern of both camps throughout the decade, they reasoned that mobilized support for the Revolution from within the United States would make an attack a harder sell to the U.S. public and would provoke widespread condemnation.

During the Civil Rights stage, the Cuban leadership sought recognition and solidarity from the Black leaders in the hope of stirring popular sentiment to lobby for a cessation of U.S. intervention. Castro had this goal in mind when visiting New York in 1960 to address the United Nations. The Cuban leadership opted to stay at the Hotel Teresa in Harlem so that they could meet with diverse Black leaders and bolster their support among the minority population. While there, Castro not only met with Malcolm X, but also with dozens of Black leaders from various political and religious backgrounds—Civil Rights leaders, Black Muslims, scholars and clergymen.[3]

At the same time, solidarity with the entire spectrum of the U.S. Black Movement would enhance the credibility of the Cuban leadership; this need for validation was paramount to the young regime throughout the 1960s and indeed is still important today. Public declarations of support for the regime from Black militants was front page news in Cuban publications; to the contrary, but not surprisingly, the press was silent when *former* sympathizers, such as Williams, Cleaver, and Carmichael, retracted their solidarity with the regime and instead expressed their unwavering devotion to the revolution's true path from which they accused Castro and the Communist Party of straying.

Public Displays of U.S. Racism

For the entire decade, sympathetic Black leaders were exemplified in the Cuban press, in speeches, and at rallies as victims of U.S. racism, oppression and capitalism. This was done in an effort to demonstrate to the world the correctness of the Cuban path and to stir nationalist fervor among Cubans for the defense and righteousness of the Revolution. The attempt at inspiring allegiance seemed particularly geared toward the Afro-Cuban population, since it was this large segment—estimated at anywhere from one-fourth to one-half of the total population[4]—more than any other, that the regime needed to convince of its dedication to the eradication of racism.[5]

Castro illustrated his regime's desire to showcase U.S. Black leaders in a speech in Havana on 30 October 1965. After describing the brutal oppression from which Williams had fled, he assured, "all those who are persecuted by reactionaries and exploiters can find asylum here."[6] At the closing of the first OLAS Conference in 1967, Castro pointed out that popular media in the U.S. was declaring that Carmichael, who was a celebrated conference participant, should not return home. The Cuban leader then shouted, "*This* country will always be his home!"[7] Malcolm's internationalist perspective regarding the Western imperialists as the true source of racism worldwide was also lauded in the Cuban press.[8]

A telephone interview with Panther leader Bobby Seale by Radio Havana was published in *Granma* shortly before Cleaver made his escape to the island. This article spotlighted the concerted efforts by U.S. police departments nationwide to destroy the Black Panther Party and gave the details of Panther member Bobby Hutton's murder and Cleaver's beating and incarceration.[9] In the early 1970s, Cuban press led the international cry to "Free Angela" Davis from her unjust imprisonment motivated by the oppression of Blacks and Communists in the United States. Upon her release, she was invited to Cuba to address thousands in Havana on the plight of the disenfranchised in the United States.[10]

Many, charging hypocrisy and maliciousness, question the regime's intentions and motivations for focusing on U.S. racial oppression while at the same time glossing over racism within Cuba. Author Carlos Moore, as well as Carmichael, Williams, and Cleaver, all expressed disillusionment with the practice of exploiting the U.S. racial issue for the regime's benefit. In retrospect, however, both Cleaver and Carmichael have concluded that the Guevarists', and Castro's, motivation with regard to this issue was well intentioned,[11] although racist and opportunistic elements did exist within the regime that created distrust toward the leadership as a whole.

BLACK LEADERS' EXPECTATIONS

Solidarity

The expectations of the African American leaders at times coalesced with the Cubans' wishes; at others, they did not, causing great confusion and frustration and leading to embarrassing breaks with the Cuban leadership. Aside from Malcolm X and King who, throughout most of their careers, did not desire a political link with the Cuban Revolution, many key leaders did seek a relationship of some sort. In general, like the Cubans, the Black leaders wanted public solidarity between themselves and the regime in order to validate their own struggle and provide support through international pressure in the event of a crisis. This solidarity was demonstrated by the Cubans in a variety of ways, but perhaps most genuinely in their acceptance into exile, despite great security risks, of fugitives Williams, Cleaver, Huey Newton, and Assata Shakur, to name a few, throughout the 1960s and 1970s.

Another way the Cubans met the expectation of solidarity was through public proclamations transmitted internationally. For example, OSPAAAL published an appeal in celebration of the International Day of Solidarity with the Black People of the U.S. in August 1967. They pledged militant solidarity and encouraged all fighters around the world to show their support in a similar way.[12] The regime also sent general messages of support through the Cuban press. But again, this militant solidarity and assistance had its limits defined by the Cuban leadership's changing ideology, security tactics, relationship with the Soviet Union and attempts at reaching a rapprochement with the U.S. government.

Another important display of Cuban solidarity with the U.S. leaders took place when Davis was accused of kidnapping, conspiracy and murder in

1970 stemming from her solidarity work with the "Soledad Brothers," three California inmates of Soledad prison who attempted to organize a Marxist study group. In late 1970, an international reaction was triggered when Davis went into hiding, was pursued and found in New York and extradited to California.[13] International protests demanding "Free Angela" arose, led most fervently by the Cubans.[14]

In the early part of the decade, it seems that given the nature of the U.S. Movement in general, Black leaders were satisfied with the solidarity demonstrated by the Cubans. Williams claimed in the early 1960s that in the future, the Black Movement might need material support, but at present, the moral support and solidarity of the socialist nations—particularly Cuba and China—was more than sufficient.[15] As will be discussed later in the context of the leaders' expectation of weapons and training that came forth from more revolutionary sectors within the U.S. Movement in the latter part of the decade, Williams' prediction was correct.

Access to the Cuban Media

U.S. Black leaders desired extensive coverage in *Granma*, the *Tricontinental* and *Tricontinental Bulletin*, and access to Radio Havana. This expectation was met to a large degree although, as discussed in chapter 4, Williams experienced serious difficulties more than any other leader, given his constant conflicts with the traditional Communist Party faction over his radio program. Nonetheless, messages of solidarity sent by the Black leaders to the Third World were made possible by these crucial media outlets; similarly, numerous Cuban organizations, including the Union of Young Communists, the Women's Federation, and the Federation of Cuban Workers, were able to demonstrate their solidarity with the militants through these media.

Arrests of Black militants, harassment, and murders were all reported around the globe via the Cuban media. While Davis was imprisoned in the United States, the Cubans waged a major media campaign to publicize her cause. The same was done for Newton and other leaders whom the Cuban press considered under attack by the U.S. government. As a result, worldwide attention was drawn to their individual plights. At the same time, by granting access to broadcast their message and stories, the Cuban media helped stir public demonstrations and international condemnation of racism against Blacks in the United States.

Access to Cuban media was significant in other ways as well: Aside from the small U.S. Black press and obscure Trotskyist newspapers like *The Militant*, the Black Movement received biased, underreported or sensationalized coverage from U.S. press. The historical record of the White-controlled media and power structure reveals their creating their own acceptable Black "leaders," co-opting the militant leaders' message through misrepresentation in the press, or demonizing and destroying them through yellow journalist tactics.[16] This biased reporting had been ongoing since the days of Booker T. Washington, W. E. B. Du Bois, and Marcus Garvey and continued through the reemerging Black Nationalist stage.

The U.S. media had been particularly ruthless in its destruction of Garvey decades earlier and tried similar tactics on Malcolm X and numerous other nationalist leaders. One tactic used by some in the mainstream media was to manipulate leaders seductively by first building them up with praise, only to make them vanish, as was the case with H. Rap Brown who replaced Carmichael as head of SNCC.[17] Under such conditions, the Cuban press provided to the Movement a much-needed outlet for the dissemination of information.

Revolutionary Violence

For various reasons, most of the leaders, including King, Malcolm X, Carmichael, and Davis, did not seek training in guerrilla tactics, weapons or explosives from the Cubans. Those who did harbor these expectations—particularly Williams, Cleaver and other members of the Black Panther Party—were largely disappointed in the Cubans' response. After 1966, the year Williams left exile in Havana, training of the U.S. militant fighters no longer was a consideration for most within the Castro regime, despite continued, fiery public statements to the contrary and promises from what appear to be renegade Guevarists stationed in New York.

As we have seen, it was against the conservative tide in Havana that, somewhere between 1967 and 1968, the Cuban government, through its liaison at the United Nations, offered an abandoned farm outside of Havana as a training facility for the Black Panthers.[18] The plan was eventually to bring clandestine squads of Panthers through Canada, Mexico or Europe to train at the Cuban facility. Four or five delegations from New York had already visited the site for a month or two at a time. But not until Cleaver was forced to flee the United States was a high-ranking Panther leader available to travel to Cuba and stay indefinitely with the aim of getting the site fully functional. The Panther leadership surmised that since Cleaver arrived in exile in late December 1968, the facility could be ready for its first trainees as early as January or February; however, many months passed and the Cubans were still stalling.[19]

On a number of occasions, the Cubans took Cleaver to the site for target practice. There he was trained with a variety of weaponry, including AK 47s, pistols, machine guns and antiaircraft weapons. His Cuban hosts also introduced him to a crew of demolition experts who would ostensibly be at the Black militants' disposal once the camp was finally in operation.[20]

Cleaver made it clear that his Party really did not need the weapons training as much as instruction in the manufacture and placement of explosives. Explosives training for the Panthers was already underway by Cuban military personnel in Canada, and the Panther leadership thought it easier and safer for the Cubans to teach them these techniques north of the border than for the trainees to travel all the way to Cuba and risk the FBI or CIA's discovering them. Still, they appreciated the Cubans' interest and pledges of support for their violent revolutionary tactics.[21]

Williams' experience was that the bulk of the Cuban regime was not willing to arm the U.S. Black Movement in the early 1960s; he expressed views similar to Cleaver's, though, indicating that this was not really of concern, since weapons were readily available throughout the United States.[22] Cleaver asserts that the Panthers never asked the Cubans for guns for that very reason. But they did request baseball-sized hand grenades, which were refused. North Korea, on the contrary, distinguished itself as a trusted supplier of these grenades, as well as AK 47s, Scorpions, and anything along this line that the Black Movement needed.[23]

After months of delays with patience running thin on both sides, the Cubans finally told Cleaver that their plan to train the militants had been abandoned. The reasons they gave were that they feared CIA or FBI infiltration of the Panthers and the U.S. Left in general and that Guevara's death put an end to the feasibility of insurrection in Latin America, not to mention in the United States.[24]

It appeared, then, that the "impending U.S. Black-led insurrection" which was still heralded in the Cuban press and still praised by Castro in his highly emotional diatribes against imperialism was betrayed by the Cuban "revolutionaries" themselves.

Granting Exile

Beginning with Williams, Cuba became home to scores of Black militant groups throughout the 1960s and 1970s. Cuba was seen by many militant fighters within the United States as a utopia, a land of which they knew little but which promised much. As the 1960s unfolded and the U.S. power structure grew more and more intolerant of racial and class militancy, Cuba became the prime destination for Black political exiles, fugitives, and those in search of freedom and equality.

It is difficult to speak definitively about the degree to which the regime fulfilled the African Americans' expectation of Cuba's harboring exiles. To its credit, throughout the decade and beyond and regardless of the increasingly cautious perspective toward the Black Movement, the regime accepted numerous desperate, and in many cases powerless, individuals. Despite the pro-Soviet faction's security and ideological positions, the Cubans granted asylum to Robert Williams in 1961, Eldridge Cleaver in 1968, Huey Newton in 1974, Assata Shakur in 1979,[25] and many others who brought little, if any, political gain to the Cuban regime. This seems to suggest that despite an erosion of political will to support a U.S. insurrection, Castro remained faithful to an ideal, which manifested itself in the harboring of exiles well beyond the point when it was to his, or Cuba's, tangible benefit.

Moreover, Williams and Cleaver, their families, and other fugitives who were approved for exile in advance of their arrival were provided with an apartment, monthly provisions of food, cigars and rum, and a housekeeper. Williams and his family were allotted a luxury apartment, and later a house, in which to live. Initially they received a living allowance and bodyguard and had a car and driver at their disposal, although these provisions were severely cut back by Communist Party members as Williams came into conflict with pro-Moscow elements who controlled his rations.[26]

This reduction in material hospitality given to Black militants became ever more prevalent as the decade progressed, as requests mounted from U.S. Blacks for help in immigrating to Cuba throughout the middle 1960s. Therefore, Williams became reluctant to offer assistance to other potential émigrés, since he sensed the trend within the traditional Communist Party camp to block any non-CPUSA activist from gaining admittance. At the same time, he was receiving more complaints from U.S. Blacks already on the island who were having difficulties with the government.[27]

The major source of contention in this realm was the treatment of hijackers. These individuals received a surprisingly hostile welcome: interrogation by Cuban intelligence followed by temporary incarceration and then forcible evacuation to a work camp. Clearly a misunderstanding occurred due, in part, to public rhetoric that showcased Cuba as a revolutionary haven for all oppressed Blacks who could get there. But behind the scenes, the regime viewed "air piracy" as a chronic security threat throughout the late 1960s and early 1970s. They came to view the Black Movement, probably accurately, as so permeated with FBI and CIA agents that trusting unknown asylum-seekers could prove quite dangerous. The Cubans therefore contended that their incarceration procedure was sound and necessary.[28]

Amuchastegui insists that the invitation to U.S. Blacks was never intended for hijackers.[29] His assertion, however, should be viewed within the context of a dwindling political will to support the U.S. Movement and the increasing intolerance of many toward hijacking. Following the purge of the Guevarists and particularly after Che's death, the desire among the Communist Party members to actively discourage hijacking gained prominence in setting policy. By 1973, the firmly Moscow-oriented regime had successfully brokered a bilateral anti-hijacking agreement with the U.S. government.

Both Cleaver and Williams conceded that some security measures needed to be taken in order to guard against counterrevolutionary forces. Nonetheless, many genuinely earnest individuals, when confronted with such harsh treatment at the hands of what they had thought to be willing and sympathetic hosts, justifiably felt disillusioned and betrayed.

A Revolutionary Society and Government

Each Black leader of course had his or her own idea as to what "revolutionary Cuba" actually entailed; not surprisingly, they encountered disappointments to varying degrees in light of their expectations of an ideal revolutionary society. The Cuban regime, therefore, failed to live up to expectations in numerous ways: (1) their rhetoric often did not reflect reality; (2) Castro and the regime were seen as abandoning the correct path outlined by Guevara; (3) a slide toward the Soviet camp and away from any sort of allowance for a racial perspective in revolutionary struggle was detected by many nationalist leaders; (4) the purging of Guevarist elements from leadership took place; (5) the regime was seen as failing to take responsibility for retreating from the march toward Communism; (6) the traditional Communist Party-dominated government to a large degree withdrew its initial support of the most militant nationalist factions and for a Black-led revolution; and (7) they displayed insensitivity, ignorance or arrogance regarding the issue of race within the United States.

The first step in the process of discovering the true nature of the revolution versus the media ideal was to dissociate the official revolutionary rhetoric—which remained consistently radical and supportive of insurrection throughout the decade—from the actual acts of solidarity taken in support of U.S. Black revolution. Williams was the first leader to discern these differences first-hand, and he did so in the very earliest years of the Cuban regime. He had learned from his own study and experiences of post-insurrectional states that continuing to employ radical slogans long after efforts at real revolutionary change had been abandoned had much historical precedent, for example, in the USSR and the United States. "This unavoidable tendency of revolutionaries once in power to become first pragmatists, then conservatives, and finally reactionaries, had affected Cuba," Williams lamented.[30]

Other leaders had similar experiences, with varying reactions. Cleaver also left Cuba, in part because of this disparity between pledges and actual actions; Carmichael questioned the revolutionary slogans in the face of an underrepresentation of Afro-Cubans in all levels of leadership; Davis, while acknowledging that Cuba had not yet achieved its goals, chose to constructively point out challenges to the regime in the hopes of bringing its actions in line with its stated aspirations.

Cleaver refutes Moore's claim that the reason for Williams' fleeing Havana was primarily racial.[31] Rather, in his own talks with Williams, he concluded that Williams' criticisms of the Cuban government were mainly ideological. Williams had clear definitions of "revolutionary" and "reactionary," and saw that Castro was making decisions that were backing away from the correct revolutionary road. Williams accused Castro of abandoning the Revolution's ideology, abandoning him, and abandoning Che Guevara.[32] While Guevara, who was ideologically close to Mao, was out of the country, Castro was scoring points with the Soviets by siding with them in their dispute with the Chinese. Williams then fled to China, which at the time was also accusing Castro of revisionism.

But this convergence with the Soviet camp was not an easy decision for the Castro regime to make, nor was it made without a price. One of the costs was a loss of revolutionary credibility in the eyes of U.S. Black leaders. The limitations placed on the Cuban regime by the Soviets, who were concerned with their détente with the United States, became apparent to the U.S. Movement. The CPUSA, in view of its domestic dispute with the Black Panthers and under Soviet guidance, tried to discourage and even disrupt relations between the Cuban Communist Party and the Black Nationalist organizations. Therefore, as CPUSA and Soviet stalwarts worldwide gained more influence in the Cuban regime, the expectation of a truly revolutionary government and society could not be fulfilled.

The "Bourgeois Communist" elements never believed that the U.S. Black Movement alone could successfully spark a nationwide armed struggle; they viewed this attempt as both dangerous and impossible given the conditions at that time.[33] Unfortunately, the first that many leaders learned of the pro-Moscow faction's true plans for their Movement was upon arrival into exile. The apparent reversal of strategy and tactics was interpreted by many as a betrayal of the U.S. Black Movement itself.

While in exile, Cleaver learned of purges in the military of those loyal to Guevara. Such acts were interpreted by him and others as a retreat from the revolutionary path. Cleaver spoke with a returning officer from Guinea-Bissau who had joined the Cuban revolutionary army under the leadership of Camilo Cienfuegos and had fought alongside Guevara. He told Cleaver that Castro's regime was sending all of the elements within the armed forces that they did not trust to Africa in order to get them out of Cuba, suppress their influence, and safeguard against a possible coup attempt.[34]

As a result of this and other actions and attitudes he discovered only after living in Cuba, Cleaver's main complaint with the regime was that it was following reactionary policies and then either denying them or justifying them through blame or scapegoating. The leadership got into the habit, he found, of blaming nearly everything negative that occurred on outside influences, usually the United States.[35] Cleaver saw this behavior as a softness in the leadership, or an inability to take responsibility for their own actions. He had learned to recognize this trait and be vigilant against it through atonement for his own criminal behavior. He discovered that only when one takes responsibility for one's role in events can anything be changed or can a real revolution continue. Cleaver also took a lesson from Mao who counseled revolutionaries to deal with their errors and shortcomings and not to hide them lest revisionism set in.[36] The Cuban leadership apparently did not have this tradition nor did they possess the fore-sight, bravery or discipline required to develop it once the revolutionary government had taken power. Guevara, who did seem to display this rig-orous judgment of self, was driven out rather than acknowledged and heeded.

The Cubans' failure to live up to this expectation exposed a flaw in the leadership of some within the U.S. Movement as well; specifically, the abil-ity of the militants to call the Cubans to task was diminished by their desire, or need, to maintain a certain political relationship with the only Communist regime in the hemisphere. For organizations such as the Black Panther Party, the example of Cuba was a beacon around which to rally the forces. Therefore, when Cleaver began sending reports back to Party head-quarters of the reactionary behavior of the regime, the persistence of racism, the petty, factional politics that were occurring, the reneging on the pledge to open the training facility, and the abandonment of support for revolutionary movements in the Americas, the Panther leadership told him to keep quiet. They said his observations were creating dissension and con-fusion in the ranks.[37]

Cleaver also alleged that David Hilliard, the acting head of the Panther Central Committee along with Bobby Seale after Newton was jailed, had come under the Stalinist influences of the CPUSA, whose support for the Cuban regime was growing in proportion to Castro's slide into the Soviet camp.[38] In the final analysis, if the Panthers did not have Cuba as an exam-ple of a revolutionary society, they were virtually isolated in the hemi-sphere; therefore, concessions were made by Newton, Hilliard, and others to the Cubans' revisionism, while those who maintained a vigilant, critical stance, such as Cleaver, were disregarded.

Another leader who railed against what he perceived as Cuban revision-ism was Stokely Carmichael. The integrationist, nonmilitant perspective of most Cuban leaders toward the U.S. Black Movement after mid-decade was not well received by the SNCC leader. Here, it is important to note two divisive elements influencing the Black militants' impression of the Cubans: First, the history of racism was perhaps more insidious, or at least more often present in national discussions and politics, in the United States than in Cuba, and therefore the threat of co-optation and betrayal by White progressives loomed large in many Black leaders' minds. The depth of this distrust was perhaps underestimated by the Cubans. Second, in the 1960s, the Chinese were bombarding California, and the United States in general, with propaganda. Mao's rhetoric was riddled with anti-White and anti-Cuban speech. Both of these factors created misgivings among Black leaders when dealing with White "revolutionaries," even those who were inhabitants of the Third World.

A Society Free of Racism

An integral part of the expectation for a revolutionary society was the hope that racism was truly eradicated in Cuba. Revolutionary Cuba was a nation without racism, Castro proudly declared. However, it is obvious that each leader's definition of racism depended greatly on a number of factors, perhaps first and foremost on whether one was Cuban or African American. In some cases, U.S. leaders could not fully understand or accept the distinct development of race relations in Cuba as it differed from the U.S. experience. So too, Cuban leaders, whether they be Castro, Guevarists, or traditional Communists, often failed to understand the racial paradigm from which the U.S. leaders' expectations sprung, and simultaneously failed to examine their own society's racism from any perspective other than their own.

The historical nature of racism in the United States differs from that in Cuba. In Cuba, to offer but one significant illustration, the struggle for independence from Spain coincided with the struggle of Blacks for liberation from slavery; in the United States, the opposite occurred: The Confederate "independence" movement was waged to a large degree *to keep Blacks enslaved*. The inability of some leaders who were oppressed under U.S. racism to judge the post-insurrectional transformation of Cuban race relations in *Cuban* terms added to the frustration of both U.S. Blacks and Cubans.

The expectation of finding in Cuba a racist-free society, although overly idealistic, was caused by the giddy ravings of Castro and other young revolutionaries who, through their optimism for the future, could not see clearly the reality of the present. They also did not anticipate the effect that their words would have on U.S. Blacks.

Another explanation for this premature announcement of a Cuban society purged of racism is offered by author Jorge Domínguez. He observes that, within the first five years of the revolution, the question of race was consciously politicized to the point where many people felt compelled to echo the claim that racism in Cuba had been eradicated and equality reigned. Although, he concludes that on balance, national integration had increased and discrimination most likely decreased, neither of these processes was complete.[39]

In the earliest years of the Revolution, racial identification or racial nationalism, along with expressing one's spirituality or individuality in general, was automatically suspect thanks largely to a prevailing and strict interpretation of Marxian teachings as well as a fervent anti-imperialist sentiment. The Cuban leadership, in response to increasing isolation from the Western world and the Americas and the rising influence of the Soviet Union, reacted by self-imposing isolation in order to build a sole Cuban Communist identity.

This manifested itself in ways that the Cuban government could control. One of these was preventing the population from physically reflecting the "hippie" influences of the United States. This took the form of prohibiting men from wearing long hair or Afro-Cubans from adopting "Afro" hairstyles similar to those of visiting foreign militants. Any divergence from the established Cuban norm was seen as nonconformist and thus counterrevolutionary. Furthermore, all types of religion, even the homegrown Afro-Cuban Santería, were banned: Santería because it was seen as nonconformist and racially nationalistic, other faiths because of disputes with the state over property rights and religious freedom, because of their siding with Batista during the insurrection, or more generally, because of the Marxian ideological bias against religion as the "opiate of the masses."

To say that these acts of government repression—particularly discouraging Afro hair styles and banning the practice of Santería—were attributable to the regime's racism is questionable given the larger context outlined above; but, Cleaver mentions two broader areas in which the Cubans failed to live up to the expectation of a racist-free society: the lack of vigilance in addressing unanswered historical racial conflicts; and the contemporary question of the distribution of power. Government proclamations and progressive laws, he observes, were not enough to erase the legacy of racism.[40] As might be expected, U.S. leaders would have different reactions to the discovery of the gulf between laws and words and to the slow pace of societal change.

Carmichael, returning in 1967 from his first trip to Cuba, attempted to dissuade Panther leaders from choosing the island as a destination for exile or training, claiming that he found the Cuban regime to be racist.[41] Although Cleaver and the Panther leadership dismissed Carmichael's allegations as the product of his own race bias, Cleaver discovered the depth of Cuban racism for himself upon his exile. Given his anticipation that some vestiges of racism would exist from prerevolutionary Cuban society, he was prepared to make allowances for their particular racial problems; as time went on, however, he realized the insidiousness of Cuban racism, tracing its historical roots to the legacy of slavery and *La Guerra Chiquita*, or "The Little War," an unsuccessful war led by the Afro-Cuban General Antonio Maceo against the Spanish colonists in 1879–80.

While in Havana, Cleaver gained access to restricted books written by and about General Maceo that were off-limits to the Cuban public. Cleaver surmised that the official denial of the rumor that Maceo was assassinated by White independence fighters out of their fear of having a Black leader was at the core of the Cuban race problem. Castro's government had neglected to address the mystery surrounding the leader's death and failed to acknowledge that many, particularly Afro-Cubans, still harbored resentment over what they deemed the official lie of an accidental slaying of Maceo on the eve of his assumption of power in Cuba.[42]

U.S. Black leaders observed that this unresolved racial issue continued to be political dynamite and was manifested in tensions and racial discrimination in the armed forces, with ramifications for all of society.[43] Many Afro-Cubans and U.S. leaders were upset that power was disproportionately concentrated in the hands of Whites despite resounding Black support for the Revolution. When asked about this issue, Amuchastegui conceded that this was a recurrent question, but answered unapologetically, "positions of leadership were held by as many Blacks as were able to distinguish themselves during the struggle against Batista."[44] Finally, the experience of the hijackers also added distrust to the relationship and created ill-will. Once released from the work camps, the shocked and disappointed individuals often spiraled further into disillusionment as they learned that racism had not, in fact, been eradicated from society: Blacks still did not hold positions of authority in proportion to their numbers, and vestiges of prerevolutionary racism were still present.

NOTES

1. Quoted in Alvarez Ríos, 435.
2. Cleaver, *Soul on Fire*, 137–43; Cleaver, interview; and "Black Power and the Revolutionary Struggle," 4–12.

3. Amuchastegui, interview.

4. Domínguez, *Cuba*, 224; and Moore, 335, 357–65.

5. See Moore, 78–82.

6. Fidel Castro, *Fidel Castro* (Havana: Instituto del Libro, 1968), 10–11.

7. Castro, "Fidel at OLAS," 2.

8. "Malcolm X, Ho Chi Minh, José Martí," *Tricontinental Bulletin*, no. 30 (September 1968): 1.

9. Bobby Seale, "Black People Must Arm to Defend Themselves," interview by Radio Havana, *Granma*, 21 April 1968, 11.

10. See *Granma*, 8 October 1972, 5.

11. Cleaver, interview; and Carmichael, letter to author, 8 October 1995.

12. "Black Power," *Tricontinental*, no. 2 (September-October 1967): 172.

13. Johnson, 75.

14. Davis, *If They Come in the Morning*, 177.

15. Cohen, 265.

16. Nathan Hare, "A Critique of Black Leaders," *Black Scholar* (March-April 1972): 3.

17. Ibid., 2–5.

18. Cleaver, interview.

19. Ibid.

20. Ibid.

21. Ibid.

22. Cohen, 298.

23. Cleaver, interview.

24. Ibid.

25. Michael Newton, 209–17; and Assata Shakur, *Assata: An Autobiography* (London: Zed Books, Ltd., 1987), 266–74.

26. Cohen, 201.

27. Ibid., 224.

28. Amuchastegui, interview; and Cleaver, interview.

29. Amuchastegui, interview.

30. Cohen, 314.

31. Cleaver, interview; and Moore, 254–56.

32. Cleaver, interview.

33. Amuchastegui, interview.

34. Cleaver, interview.

35. Ibid.

36. Ibid.

37. Ibid.

38. Ibid.

39. Domínguez, *Cuba*, 478–85.

40. Cleaver, interview.

41. Ibid.

42. Ibid.
43. Ibid.
44. Amuchastegui, interview.

THE DECLINE OF THE RADICAL ALLIANCE

The convergence of a number of factors resulted in a change in the nature of Cuba's relationship with the U.S. Black Movement at the end of the decade that continued into the 1970s. Among these factors were a shift in the ideologies of the Black leaders themselves, a splintering of militant organizations that weakened the Movement, the ultimate dominance of the Cuban traditional Communist Party faction over the Guevarists in setting policy, the changing Cuban political strategy away from insurrection in the Americas and toward an African focus, and Washington's disengagement from the Vietnam conflict.

CHANGING IDEOLOGIES OF INDIVIDUAL BLACK LEADERS

As the decade closed and the 1970s began, Williams and Cleaver floundered in obscurity and self-questioning in exile. Back home, the Black Panther Party platform and leadership were becoming more conciliatory and reformist. Yet other leaders, like Carmichael, were increasingly drawn to the anticolonial struggles of Africa. Their ideologies, consequently, developed into a Pan-Africanist perspective whereby the revolution had first to take hold on African soil. This internationalization of the struggle and the shift in focus away from the Americas coincided with Cuba's escalation of military involvement in Africa. Cuban soldiers fighting alongside Africans in the Congo and Angola garnered much respect and solidarity from Blacks all over the world, including new sectors of the U.S. population.

The decline of the Black Panther Party and Black Nationalism in general can be attributed to several factors: The relentless attacks by the U.S. government using violence, intimidation and infiltration through the FBI's COINTELPRO and later the NEWKILL program under the leadership of Hoover and involving local police departments; serious internal power struggles and organizational errors; the lack of mass support within the Black community for the militants' violent tactics and radical strategies; the consequent new directions that the militant factions were taking—some reformist and others radically separatist—which exacerbated the breakdown; and a fundamental crisis in leadership that pervaded the entire Movement.

The rampant infiltration of the radical ranks has been well documented.[1] Earl Anthony, an FBI informant planted in the Oakland, California, Panther Party, stated that the Panthers were influenced as much by Communists as they were by FBI agents.[2] As early as 1969, it is believed that between sixty and seventy infiltrators were among the membership in the Bay Area of California, and these rates of infiltration were consistent with those of other groups such as SNCC.[3]

The technique of "badjacketing," or spreading false information about a dedicated member in order to plant seeds of mistrust, was widely practiced. FBI documents reveal that Carmichael was the target of successful badjacketing, leading to an allegation by the Panthers in 1970 that he was a CIA agent.[4] Through obtaining his own FBI file, Cleaver has discovered falsified letters in his name that were sent to Huey Newton, Kathleen Cleaver, his wife at the time, and others, attempting to create distrust and bitterness both among the Panther leadership and within his marriage.[5]

Aside from government meddling, internal Party conflicts were coming to a head by late decade. When Newton was released from prison in August 1970, dramatic and destructive changes had been brewing within the Party, characterized by a New York/Oakland split. Tensions flared over the New York 21, also known as the Panther 21, who were charged with conspiring to bomb police stations and department stores and murder police officers. The 21 issued a statement in support of a manifesto by the Weather Underground calling for armed conflict. David Hilliard, acting head of the Panthers in Oakland while Newton was incarcerated, denounced the defendants' move for not first clearing their statement with him. Cleaver, who was in exile in Algiers, sided with the New York 21; Newton, upon release from jail, supported Hilliard. Newton also accused the members of the East Coast contingent of plotting to assassinate him, as many were unhappy with his and Hilliard's leadership.[6]

In early 1971 the U.S. media became aware of the split and set up a trans-Atlantic debate between the two party leaders. The result was Newton's ex-communicating the Black Panther Party International (Cleaver's group in Algeria) and, in turn, the committee members' in Algiers ex-communicating Newton.[7] Fighting words turned into fighting actions culminating in internal murders and arson in the New York headquarters that spring. These actions, accompanied by thorough going purges of renegade members and suspected government infiltrators, had disastrous effects on Party morale, participation and ideological development.

Cleaver also acknowledged that the clash of egos, the oppression of women within the organization and issues of sex were a severe handicap for the group. Female Party members had to struggle for recognition, the right to vote and equal, nonharassing treatment from their supposedly revolutionary brothers. Coups d'état attempts were frequent, as different members competed to gain power, economic advantage and ego satisfaction. These attitudes and actions were carried outside the Party organization as well, as groups vied for the attention of the Cubans and the media. A climate of hostility and competition prevailed where statements would be issued and political maneuverings undertaken that would help one's image while simultaneously hurting one's enemies, who were often within the same organization.[8]

The combined effect of these factors was successful in achieving the FBI's goals of destroying the Movement internally, discrediting or eliminating effective Black leadership and isolating the various groups from one another and from the international struggle. In the process, over 300 Black men were reportedly killed, most of whom were members of Cleaver's faction. According to Earl Anthony, 95 percent of the murders were committed by fellow Panthers accusing one another of being FBI or police informers.[9]

By 1975, the original Black Panther leadership had been removed from power: Cleaver, after a disillusioning eight years in exile, had turned to creative writing and evangelistic Christianity; Newton was in exile in Havana; and Bobby Seale was advocating mainstream political reform. The Cubans, who had long since abandoned any hopes of a Black-led U.S. insurrection and who were firmly within the Soviet camp, turned to embrace the solidarity from other, more mild, sectors of the U.S. Black population, who were drawn to Cuba for the shared African heritage.

TRIUMPH OF THE TRADITIONAL COMMUNIST PARTY

The primary reason for the decline in the Cuban regime's attention to the U.S. Movement has been echoed throughout this work: The struggle between the Guevarist and the pro-Moscow camps to chart the course of the Revolution, influenced Castro's decision making and set policy toward the Black Movement resulted in the dominance by mid-decade of the traditional Communist Party. This faction, for the variety of reasons discussed throughout, took an ideological and security stance most often at odds with the U.S. Black militants' viewpoints and expectations. As the "Bourgeois Communists" gained influence and forced the Guevarists, sympathetic to the U.S. radicals, from power, Soviet recommendations to halt the "export" of revolution were heeded, and material support for the Black militants ceased. Che's dream of creating many Vietnams in the Americas, however, needed to be soundly defeated before Castro would entirely abandon the Guevarist insurrectional tactics and strategy.

CHANGING CUBAN POLITICAL STRATEGY

Cuba's final shift in attention away from the Americas and toward Africa was primarily due to the failures of Guevara's guerrilla "foco" tactics in Latin America. The first major defeat occurred in Argentina in 1963–64 after an endeavor led by Jorge Masetti but planned by Guevara.[10] Che made a final attempt to implement the "foco" theory in Bolivia three years later, an effort which ended in his capture and death. Soon after, the indiscriminate "two, three, many Vietnams" battle cry was rendered insupportable, and the Cubans ceased promoting guerrilla-led insurrectional rhetoric throughout the Third World. In addition, any spill over propaganda in support of a Black-led U.S. insurrection disappeared from the Cuban media. This, of course, was years after the regime had begun discreetly discouraging such a goal among Black leaders in exile.

Cuba's involvement in Africa, while beyond the scope of this book, coincided with an upsurge in cultural and political interest in the continent on the part of U.S. Black leaders. This combination brought about a decided shift in the type of African American leaders with whom Cuba would develop relations. Cultural and religious leaders, intellectuals and artists would now receive Cuba's attention. The Cuban military involvement in Africa unexpectedly provided the regime with renewed respect and solidarity from diverse U.S. Black leaders throughout the late seventies, establishing a rapport that continues to this day.

U.S. DISENGAGEMENT FROM VIETNAM

The U.S. withdrawal from Vietnam effectively ended the large U.S. Anti-War Movement in which Cuba saw the possibility of forcing a profound change in U.S. interventionist policies. Since, in the Cubans' view, the Black Movement would be most effectual if it could mobilize the Black community to rally against the war in Vietnam, its role was now nullified. And given the unpopularity of the war and the prevention of a decisive victory for the United States, the Cubans felt that their sovereignty was, to a degree, secured. The war-weary U.S. populace most likely would not tolerate further aggression against another small Third World country, or so the regime hoped. Finally, as minority-led insurrection became less and less acceptable to the Cuban leadership after the ascension of the conservative pro-Soviets and the failure of the Bolivian experiment, support for Black revolutionary nationalists waned.

NOTES

1. See Ward Churchill and Jim Vander Wall, *Agents of Repression* (Boston: South End Press, 1990); Churchill, *The COINTELPRO Papers*; and Cathy Perkus, ed., *COINTELPRO: The FBI's Secret War on Political Freedom* (New York: Monad Press, 1975).
2. Quoted in Michael Newton, 225.
3. Churchill and Vander Wall, 48.
4. Ibid., 49.
5. Cleaver, interview.
6. Ibid.
7. Ibid.
8. Ibid.
9. Quoted in Michael Newton, 229–30.
10. Rojo, 147–62.

CONCLUSION

Relations between the Cuban government and African American leaders throughout the 1960s were complex, sometimes mutually beneficial and oftentimes turbulent, but always affected by the plethora of diverse political voices entering the debate and vying for dominance. The most important determinant in these relations was the power struggle between two opposing camps within the Cuban regime, the Guevarist faction, loyal to Ernesto "Che" Guevara's internationalist revolutionary philosophy, and the traditional Community Party faction, many of whom had been high-ranking leaders of the pre-insurrection Popular Socialist Party and continued to take directives from the Kremlin after the Revolution triumphed.

At the same time that the pacifist Civil Rights phase of the U.S. Movement gave way to the militant Black Nationalist phase, the Cuban regime was moving in an opposite direction. The Guevarist faction, sympathetic toward the U.S. Black radicals, was successfully isolated from power by mid-decade as the traditional Communist Party camp gained favor with Fidel Castro. The net effect of the rise of the pro-USSR faction and the island's escalating military and economic dependence on the Soviet Union was the adoption by late decade of a Moscow-oriented security policy and ideological stance, ultimately signaling the demise of any significant relations with the ascending U.S. Black militants.

Defining the first two stages of the modern U.S. Black Movement—which coincided with the first decade of the Cuban Revolution—helps in understanding the context in which these relations developed. The first stage examined in this book, namely, Civil Rights (1950s–1965), witnessed the nonviolent philosophy of Dr. Martin Luther King, Jr., which contrasted sharply with those of other more militant voices. The Black Muslim Malcolm X and Robert Williams, both of whom advocated armed self-defense and, later, insurrection in order to achieve Black liberation, were forerunners of the Black Nationalist stage of the second part of the decade.

Black Nationalism (1965–early 1970s) embodied a number of distinct nationalist sentiments, including cultural nationalism, Pan-Africanism, Black Power, and revolutionary nationalism. Defining these significant strains of Black Nationalism is essential if prominent militant leaders of the time—Stokely Carmichael (Kwame Ture) of the Student Non-Violent Coordinating Committee (SNCC), Eldridge Cleaver of the Black Panther Party for Self-Defense, and Angela Davis of the Communist Party USA (CPUSA)—are to be viewed in their respective political frameworks. These dispositions provide background for comparing their ideologies and tactics with those of the Cuban factions.

The international context in which the Cuban-U.S. Black relations developed shows that Soviet-Cuban relations, as they affected Cuban support for U.S. militants, hinged on the two issues of ideology and national security. Castro wavered between the Guevarist camp and the pro-Soviet faction on these crucial concerns throughout the decade. His fluctuations translated into erratic policy toward the U.S. Black Movement. Inextricable from this discussion is the issue of relations with the U.S. government. The traditional Communist Party faction successfully lobbied its more conservative position with Castro around mid-decade, while the Guevarist philosophy of actively promoting revolution throughout the hemisphere was deemed untenable. Thus, Cuba gained the benefits of Soviet patronage, which afforded it protection and a degree of economic stability but at the expense of an independent, revolutionary ideology and security policy.

The Sino-Soviet split allowed the Cubans a brief opportunity in the early 1960s to gain a better bargaining position with the USSR and won for the Cuban regime more room to maneuver politically. But by late decade, China moved toward rapprochement with the U.S. government and Cuba slid into the Soviet camp, with the result that Cuban support for insurrection in the Americas significantly dwindled.

The conflict in Vietnam also played a considerable role in defining Cuban-U.S. Black relations. The Cuban regime found encouragement in the mounting anti-interventionist U.S. Peace Movement and was hopeful that the protracted conflict could make a U.S. invasion of the island less likely. As a means to achieve this goal, the Cubans sought contacts with Black leaders who could effectively lead African Americans into the larger Anti-War Movement.

The reemergence of an internationalist view of struggle within the Black Movement was apparent among all leaders, from King to Cleaver. Linking the oppression of people of color everywhere—Africans, U.S. Blacks, Cubans, and the Vietnamese—was a common theme throughout the 1960s that drew U.S. Blacks closer to the Cuban regime and people. Although the active promotion of the Cuban revolutionary example, or at least some variation of it, was designated by the Guevarist camp to be a primary goal of Cuban foreign policy, the pro-Moscow faction retreated from this precarious role by mid-decade. Just as support for an armed insurrection grew among U.S. Blacks through the latter half of the decade, those Cubans who were most willing to support it, the Guevarists, were driven from power. Nonetheless, the combination of an increasingly internationalist perspective among U.S. Blacks and the active support by Havana for decolonization in Africa and Asia granted the Cuban regime much respect from many of the fledgling African countries as well as from the U.S. militants.

The reasons for divergent or convergent relations among individual leaders can be clarified by contrasting the distinct ideologies and tactics of the Cuban traditional Communist Party faction, the Guevarist faction, Fidel Castro, and the U.S. Black leaders, including Williams, King, Malcolm X, Carmichael, Cleaver, and Davis. Ideologically, the leaders and factions either converged or clashed with one another on the basis of the following considerations: (1) whether they were segregationist or integrationist; (2) whether they were nationalist, and if so, what type; (3) whether they displayed elements of racism, defined as believing that one race is superior to another, advocating discrimination or holding racially prejudiced views; (4) whether they advanced a race and/or class analysis; and (5) whether they advocated violence.

As the decade progressed, it was demonstrated that ideological convergence with Castro or Guevara in no way assured the Black leaders of positive relations with regard to the regime as a whole; rather, as the pro-Moscow faction gained ideological dominance, nationalist leaders lost favor with the regime and a strict, class-based and largely nonviolent analysis of the U.S. struggle was promoted by the Cuban Communist Party. Some radical leaders, such as Williams, Cleaver, and Carmichael, lamented the loss of Guevara's influence over Cuban ideology, because the Guevarists did not reject Black nationalist sentiment outright and also actively promoted revolutionary violence. These leaders felt that the Cuban Revolution and, consequently, the impending U.S. Black-led insurrection were being betrayed by revisionist and reactionary elements within the regime.

The issue of security—both the Black leaders' individual safety concerns and Cuba's national security—was decided by the outcome of the struggle to set policy that raged between the two Cuban factions throughout the first half of the decade. The traditional Communist Party faction, which eventually won out, sought to move Cuba into the Soviet camp for protection and economic stability. The Guevarists, by contrast, lobbied for assisting in the forceful overthrow of the world capitalist system in order ultimately to safeguard the island's security without sacrificing its independent, revolutionary path.

The U.S. threat to Cuban security was most starkly displayed in the 1961 Bay of Pigs invasion and the October Missile Crisis the following year. Yet hostilities continued throughout the Johnson and Nixon administrations, raising the stakes and intensifying the debate over security policy within the Cuban regime. In spite of Washington's continued suspicion of significant links between the Black Movement and the Castro regime—suspicion that led to a CIA investigation in 1969 and 1970—the traditional Communist Party faction had, by that time, already successfully sidelined relations with the U.S revolutionaries. By the latter part of the decade, any real act on the part of the regime beyond paying lip service to "international solidarity" was negligible.

Addressing Black leaders' personal safety concerns within the fluctuations of Cuban security policy was in many ways a difficult task. Every U.S. Black leader faced a threat to his or her personal safety, as illustrated in the harassment and eventual assassinations of King and Malcolm X. The FBI, for its part, launched a massive counterintelligence program (COINTEL-PRO) in 1968 in an effort to break the Black Nationalist organizations. Therefore, as desperate exiles fled to Cuba seeking shelter in that allegedly revolutionary and sympathetic state, the debate between the Guevarists and the pro-Soviets over the most prudent national security strategy was thrown into sharp relief. The limits to Cuban solidarity were tested throughout the decade by such revolutionary nationalists seeking exile as Robert Williams and Black Panthers Eldridge Cleaver, Huey Newton, and Assata Shakur.

The exile experiences of Williams and Cleaver illustrate the erratic shifts in Cuban policy toward the U.S. Movement. In the end, both of these leaders left Cuba for other exile destinations, citing a betrayal of revolutionary ideals by powerful Communist Party stalwarts. Far from the omnipotent and omnipresent leader that he is usually considered to be, Castro, according to Williams and Cleaver, was kept from knowing what was transpiring in relations with Black militants by the reactionary elements within the regime.

These leaders' falling-out with the Cubans was due in large part to divergent expectations of one another. Cuban expectations of Black leadership changed little throughout the decade and depended primarily on which Cuban faction held more influence in setting policy; the nature of the U.S. Black leadership itself was of much less import. Cuban expectations included the hope that the African Americans would merge their struggle with the larger Anti-War Movement; that by offering solidarity to the regime, they would enhance Cuban credibility while possibly deterring a U.S. invasion; and that victims of U.S. racism (Black leaders) could be publicly displayed to the Cuban people in an effort to prove the superiority of the Revolution. Each of these expectations was met to a significant degree by a number, although not all, of the Black leaders discussed.

The African American leaders' expectations included solidarity with the regime, which was genuinely fulfilled by the Guevarist faction and at least officially met by the traditional Communist Party faction; access to Cuban media in order to broadcast their message throughout the world, which was met in full, with the exception of Williams' radio program being shut down; assistance in revolutionary violence (training and weapons), an expectation that was for the most part unrealized, with the exception of a brief training of Black Panther Party members; and the granting of exile which was complied with fully and long after it seemed politically beneficial for the regime to do so.

Two final expectations—that in Cuba there existed a truly revolutionary society and leadership and that it was a country free of racism—were much more problematic. Disappointment and anger often surfaced after the discovery that racism persisted despite official assurances to the contrary. The combination of a burgeoning Soviet-like bureaucracy, dwindling official support for insurrection, and the lack of personal freedoms in Cuban society threw into question the revolutionary ideal toward which many Black leaders were struggling. With the exception of Davis, all of the leaders who had experienced first hand Cuba's society and regime, that is, Williams, Carmichael, and Cleaver, concluded that Cuba fell far short of their expectations regarding these two important issues.

The forces that contributed to the decline of Cuba's attention to the U.S. Black radicals were many. Again, the most crucial factor in this decline of alliances was the triumph of the traditional Communist Party forces over the Guevarists around mid-decade, just as Black Nationalism was gaining momentum in the U.S. struggle. Nonetheless, unrelated events in the United States, including evolving ideologies of individual leaders and the fracturing of the U.S. militant organizations through both internal breakdown and the FBI's COINTELPRO, worked to diffuse the Nationalist movement.

In Cuba, the routing of the Guevarists from political power was followed by the ultimate defeat of the guerrilla "foco" experiment in Bolivia in 1967, an event that seemed to put to rest many Cubans' hopes, including Castro's, for hemispheric insurrection. The idea of minority-led revolution in Latin America, much less the United States, became practically a non-issue after the ascension of the pro-Soviets and Guevara's death. Cuba's international focus then turned to the decolonization struggles in Africa, which had the effect of winning for the regime new and more moderate sympathizers within the African American community.

Finally, the U.S. disengagement from Vietnam brought an end to the Anti-War Movement, in which the Cubans had seen the prospect of achieving profound change in Washington's interventionist actions. Since the traditional Communist Party faction perceived that the primary role of Black militant leaders was to merge their struggle with the larger Peace Movement, their function was nullified. Each of these factors contributed to the decline in the latter half of the 1960s of the Cuba-U.S. Black radical alliance.

REVOLUTIONARY VIGILANCE VERSUS REACTIONARY RATIONALIZATION

The examination of the relations among militant, and often revolutionary, leadership over the course of a decade points to some general conclusions about revolutionary leaders and proximity to power. The outcome of the power struggle between the Guevarist and traditional Communist Party factions in Cuba suggests that when decisions are made in revolutionary situations based on maintaining or bettering one's own proximity to power or that of one's group, then revisionism and reactionary policies often take root. Comfort, excuses, and maintaining status come to replace bravery, conviction and international solidarity, as witnessed in the ascending pro-Moscow faction's perception of, and lack of dedication to, the U.S. Black revolutionary nationalists. The triumph of the traditional Communists over the Guevarists may be viewed, then, as a triumph of the mere safeguarding of a regime over revolutionary progress.

Che Guevara's ideal of the revolutionary man and woman, as put forth in *Socialism and Man in Cuba*,[1] was intuitively shared by Black revolutionary thinkers in North America. Leaders like Malcolm X, Robert Williams, Eldridge Cleaver, Stokely Carmichael, and Angela Davis had similar conceptions of how the revolutionary individual and society might be constructed. They too had to make decisive choices between a path of "less resistance" which would assure at least survival and at best a degree of comfort and international prestige, or the uncharted, lonely, dangerous, and personally conceived revolutionary path.

Black leaders who were embraced by the Cubans had to remain vigilant in their revolutionary thinking and behavior lest they succumb to the seductive role of militant celebrity in exile or anachronistic, and so permissible, social critic at home. Williams and Cleaver, the leaders discussed in this book who sought exile in Cuba, resisted the temptation of co-optation and held true to their own convictions. They continued searching for a truly revolutionary society and regime, one that embraced both an understanding of class *and* race.

It could be argued that Carmichael, who initially rejected the Cuban regime because of its alleged racism, became less critical in his assessment after assuming a leadership role in African politics, since Cuba was one of the few supporters of the recently decolonized countries of that continent. It could also be concluded that Davis, as a prominent CPUSA leader, has chosen to restrain her criticisms of the regime in light of her desire to maintain status within the Communist Party structure worldwide. What seems more likely, however, based on Davis and Carmichael's decades-long commitment to a revolutionary path and to the Cuban regime, is that they reserve their concerns for private and constructive dialogues aimed at improving and furthering the Revolution overall.

RACE VERSUS CLASS ANALYSIS

The traditional Soviet model of revolution and governance has never adequately allowed for the issues of racial oppression or distinction. Malcolm X, Williams, Carmichael, Cleaver, and even Davis (through the Che-Lumumba collective of the CPUSA) voiced their concerns over the limitations of applying a European, class-based analysis to the contemporary U.S. situation. Guevara, others within the 26th of July Movement, and many Afro-Cubans shared this understanding with the U.S. Black leaders and encouraged efforts at adapting Marxism-Leninism to the nationalist struggle within the United States.

However, as the pro-Soviets drove the Guevarists from power around mid-decade, a stale and rigid form of class analysis won out, making relations with the increasingly radical Black Nationalists tenuous at best. In the face of this narrow consciousness, most Black leaders balked. Williams held firm to his convictions and dedication to Black liberation and fled to China in search of revolutionary support and a society free of racism. Cleaver had a similar response when he met with continuous delays in beginning military training of Black Panthers on the island. His flight to Algiers, followed by his widely publicized criticisms of the Revolution, did not so much signify disillusionment with a socialist path as it did a rage against human softness and less-than-revolutionary leadership.

Carmichael, like Malcolm X, harbored a deep distrust and resentment toward Whites, and therefore his initial break with the Cubans over their alleged racism was not so surprising. What was more unexpected was his all-out embracing of the Cuban Revolution and leadership following his self-imposed exile in the Republic of Guinea, West Africa, in the late 1960s. In a marked departure from his views of that era, today Carmichael states that the Cubans have actively fought racism in their own society and around the world and continue to fight it today. Additionally, he, along with Davis, still believes that African Americans will be the spark for the impending U.S. revolution leading to a socialist society.[2]

REVOLUTIONARY VIOLENCE

That many within the Cuban regime ever believed that the U.S. Black revolutionaries could in fact lead a successful insurrection in "the belly of the beast" is certainly debatable; it seems most plausible that the traditional

Communists thought it highly unlikely and even putschist to attempt at all. Such a response could readily be attributed to their rejection of ethnic nationalism as a legitimate basis for struggle and to their conservative views on violent agitation in the hemisphere which bowed to Soviet dictates.

But the Guevarists and many within the 26th of July Movement as well as Castro himself, for a time, seemed to have at least attempted to pursue this avenue as far as it would go. The training of Black Panther Party members and other radical groups in Canada by Cuban military in the late 1960s illustrates this commitment to revolutionary violence in the United States. The pledge made—surely in full consultation with Castro—by a Cuban representative at the UN to give weapons and explosives training to Panthers at a site outside of Havana[3] further demonstrates their conviction.

Despite the Cubans' intentions, a combination of factors prevented any significant military support. First and foremost, the pro-Moscow faction quickly gained control of security policy and ideology, which halted anything but official, verbal support for a Black nationalist-led insurrection. Second, the Guevarist campaign for hemispheric guerrilla warfare was proving unsuccessful and costly on every front, and therefore the likelihood of insurrection in the United States seemed every day more remote. Third, the Black Movement itself was suffering from internal breakdown for a variety of reasons, and by the close of the decade, stagnation and fatigue had replaced the momentum of only a few months earlier. This loss of momentum was inextricably linked to the de-escalation of the Vietnam War, which brought about a diminution in the radical Peace Movement and, in turn, a subsiding of the Cubans' attention to the United States vis-à-vis radical political change in general.

By 1968, the Cubans had reneged on their offer to give the Panthers a training facility outside of Havana, were promoting to the Black Movement an integrationist approach of nonviolent agitation to be carried out in cooperation with White U.S. workers, and no longer had any real intention nor desire to fund, train, or arm the Movement. Cleaver stated that only the North Koreans consistently demonstrated their willingness to support the U.S. Black insurrectional struggle with weapons and explosives.[4]

As Carmichael recently remarked, usually comrades, or allies, do not fall out over strategic or tactical differences, but over principles, even though these principles may be hidden from one another and even from oneself.[5] If he is correct, it appears that principles dictated where the Cuban-U.S. Black alliances either broke down or were maintained. In the opinion of

Williams and Cleaver, the principles for which Guevara lived and died were no longer valued by the traditional Communist Party faction, and consequently a rift developed not only between the Cuban factions but between the Black leaders and the Cuban government. Carmichael and Davis, on the other hand, managed to find common ground with the Cuban regime throughout the decades thanks, in part, to shared principles and beliefs. For Davis, it is a general adherence to a Marxist-Leninist doctrine; for Carmichael, it is a mutual struggle for the liberation of Africa from European influence. The principles to which a potential ally adheres are—like Fidel himself—often difficult to grasp, influence, negotiate with, or overpower. And principles, along with loyalty to them, were perhaps the fundamental factor in the ebb and flow of Cuban-U.S. Black alliances throughout the 1960s.

NOTES

1. Ernesto "Che" Guevara, *Socialism and Man in Cuba* (New York: Pathfinder Press, 1989).
2. Carmichael, letter to author, 8 October 1995.
3. Cleaver, interview.
4. Ibid.
5. Carmichael, letter to author, 8 October 1995.

BIBLIOGRAPHY

Abraham, Kinfe. *Politics of Black Nationalism: From Harlem to Soweto.* Trenton, N.J.: Africa World Press, Inc., 1991.

Abron, JoNina M. "The Legacy of the Black Panther Party." *The Black Scholar* (November–December 1968): 33–37.

Allen, Robert. "Black Liberation and World Revolution." *The Black Scholar* (February 1972): 7–23.

Alvarez Ríos, Baldomero, ed. Cuba: Revolución e imperialismo [Cuba: Revolution and Imperialism]. Havana: Instituto del Libro, 1969.

Amuchastegui, Domingo. Interview by author. Tape Recording. Miami, Fla., 23 March 1995. Formerly an official in the Cuban Ministry of Foreign Affairs, Intelligence, and the head of the Department of Organization vis-à-vis the Tricontinental organizations during the 1960s and 1970s.

Anderson, Jon Lee. *Che Guevara: A Revolutionary Life.* New York: Grove Press, 1997.

Anthony, Earl. *Picking Up the Gun.* New York: Pyramid Books, 1970.

Archivo Nacional de Cuba. *Documentos para servir a la historia de la Guerra Chiquita* [Documents to Serve the History of the Little War]. Havana: Archivo Nacional de Cuba, 1949–1950.

Balagoon, Kuwasi et al. *Look For Me in the Whirlwind: The Collective Autobiography of the New York 21.* New York: Random House, 1971.

Baloyra, Enrique A., and James A. Morris, eds. *Conflict and Change in Cuba.* Albuquerque: University of New Mexico Press, 1993.

Bernard, Sheila, and Sam Pollard. "The Time has Come (1964–1966)." *Eyes on the Prize II.* PBS Home Video. Boston: Blackside, Inc., 1990.

Berry, Mary Frances, and John W. Blassingame. *Long Memory—The Black Experience in America*. New York: Oxford University Press, 1982.

Biblioteca Nacional José Martí. *Bibliografía de la Guerra Chiquita, 1879–1880* [Bibliography of the Little War, 1879–1880]. Havana: Instituto del Libro, 1975.

"Black Power." *Tricontinental* (Havana), no. 2 (September–October 1967): 172.

"Black Power and the Revolutionary Struggle." *Tricontinental Bulletin* (Havana), no. 32 (November 1968): 4–12.

Boggs, James. "Black Revolutionary Power." *Ebony* (August 1970): 152–55.

Bohemia (Havana), 23 December 1966.

Bracey, John H., Jr., August Meier, and Elliott Rudwick, eds. *Black Nationalism in America*. New York: The Bobbs-Merrill Company, Inc., 1970.

Brent, William Lee. *Long Time Gone*. New York: Random House, 1996.

Carlisle, Rodney. *The Roots of Black Nationalism*. Port Washington, N.Y.: Kennikat Press Corp., 1975.

Carmichael, Stokely [Kwame Ture]. Letters to author, 15 and 21 June 1995, 8 October 1995.

_____. "Marxism-Leninism and Nkrumahism." *The Black Scholar* (February 1973): 41–43.

_____. "Pan-Africanism-Land and Power." *The Black Scholar* (November 1969): 36–43.

_____. *Stokely Speaks: Black Power to Pan-Africanism*. New York: Random House, 1971.

Carmichael, Stokely, and Charles V. Hamilton. *Black Power: The Politics of Liberation in America*. New York: Random House, 1967.

Carson, Clayborne. *In Struggle: SNCC and the Black Awakening of the 1960s*. Cambridge: Harvard University Press, 1981.

_____. *Malcolm X: The FBI File*. New York: One World Books, 1995.

Castro, Fidel. "Algunos problemas de los métodos y formas de trabajo de las ORI" [Some Problems of the Methods and Functioning of the ORI). *Obra Revolucionaria* (Havana) 10 (1962): 7–32.

_____. *Angola girón african*. Havana; Editorial de Ciencias Sociales, 1976.

_____. *Fidel Castro*. Havana: Instituto del Libro, 1968.

_____. *Fidel Castro: Discours de la Revolution* [Speech on the Revolution]. Edited by Christine Glucksmann. Paris: Union Generale d'Editions, 1966.

_____. *Fidel Castro Speaks*. Edited by Martin Kenner and James Petras. Harmondsworth: Penguin Books, 1972.

_____. Letter to Celia Sanchez. 5 June 1958. Pp. 473 in *Diario de la Revoluciia Sanche* [Diary of the Cuban revolution], ed. Carlos Franqui. Paris: Ruedo Ibérico, 1976.

_____. Second Declaration of Havana. *Comisión Cubana en la ONU*, 1968.

_____. "Statement by Fidel Castro at the Solemn Tribute in Havana." *Tricontinental*, no. 2 (September–October 1967): 105–16.

Castro, Fidel, and Ernesto "Che" Guevara. *To Speak the Truth*. Edited by Mary-Alice Waters. New York: Pathfinder Press, 1992.

Central Intelligence Agency. *The Inspector General's Survey of the Cuban Operation* (Washington, D.C.: The National Security Archive, 1961). Document available at the archive's web site: http://www.seas.gwu.edu/nsarchive.

Chrisman, Robert, and Robert L. Allan. "The Cuban Revolution: Lessons for the Third World." *The Black Scholar* (February 1973): 2–14.

Churchill, Ward, and Jim Vander Wall. *Agents of Repression*. Boston: South End Press, 1990.

_____. *The COINTELPRO Papers*. Boston: South End Press, 1990.

Clark, Steve. "A Reply to Lies in the *New York Times* on Che and the Cuban Revolution." *Militant* 59, no. 47 (7 December 1995): ISR/5.

Cleaver, Eldridge. *Eldridge Cleaver: Post-Prison Writings and Speeches*. New York: Random House, 1969.

_____. "Fidel Castro's African Gambit." *Newsweek* (3 May 1976): 13.

_____. Interview by author. Tape recording. Miami, Fla., 20 January and 11 February 1996.

_____. "On Lumpen Ideology." *The Black Scholar* (November–December 1972): 2–10.

_____. *Soul on Fire*. Waco, Tex.: World Books, 1978.

_____. *Soul on Ice*. New York: Dell Publishing Co., 1968.

Clissold, Stephen. *Soviet Relations with Latin America, 1918–1968*. New York: Oxford University Press, 1970.

Clytus, John, with Jane Rieker. *Black Man in Red Cuba*. Coral Gables, Fla.: University of Miami Press, 1970.

Cohen, Robert Carl. *Black Crusader: A Biography of Robert Franklin Williams*. Secaucus, N.J.: Lyle Stuart, Inc., 1972.

Cole, Johnnetta B. *The Black Scholar* (November–December 1980): 2–24.

_____. *Race Toward Equality*. Havana: José Martí Publishing House, 1986.

"Communist Threat to the US through the Caribbean." Hearings before the Subcommittee to Investigate the Administration of the Internal Security Act, etc., of the Committee of the Judiciary. U.S. Senate, 86th Congress, First Session, 5 November 1959.

Crankshaw, Edward, ed. *Khrushchev Remembers*. Boston: Little, Brown & Co., 1970.

Davis, Angela Yvonne. *Angela Davis: An Autobiography*. New York: Random House, 1988.

_____. *If They Come in the Morning: Voices of Resistance*. New York: Third Press, 1971.

_____. *Women, Race and Class*. New York: Random House, 1983.

Debray, Regis. *Revolution in the Revolution?* New York: Monthly Review Press, 1967.

Domínguez, Jorge I. *Cuba: Order and Revolution*. Cambridge: Harvard University Press, 1978.

_____. *To Make a World Safe for Revolution*. Cambridge: Harvard University Press, 1989.

Draper, Theodore. *Castro's Revolution: Myths and Realities*. New York: Praeger, 1962.

"Editorial." *Tricontinental*, no. 2 (September–October 1967): np.

"Editorial." *Tricontinental*, no. 10 (January–February 1969): np.

Falk, Pamela S. *Cuban Foreign Policy: Caribbean Tempest*. Lexington, Mass.: Lexington Books, 1986.

Federal Bureau of Investigation. Affidavit dated 28 September 1963 by Karl Prussian. FBI File # 100–106670, Section 13, 22 July 1964.

Foner, Philip S. *The Black Panthers Speak*. Philadelphia: J.B. Lipponcott Co., 1970.

Franklin, John Hope. *From Slavery to Freedom*. New York: Alfred A. Knopf, Inc., 1967.

_____, August Meier, eds. *Black Leaders of the Twentieth Century*. Champaign: University of Illinois Press, 1982.

Franklin, V.P. *Black Self-Determination*. Westport, Conn.: Lawrence Hill & Company, 1984.

Franqui, Carlos. *Diario de la Revolución cubana* [Diary of the Cuban Revolution]. Paris: Ruedo Ibérico, 1976.

Galeano, Eduardo. *Open Veins of Latin America*. New York: Monthly Review Press, 1973.

Garrow, J. David. *The FBI and Martin Luther King, Jr. From "Solo" to Memphis*. W.W. Norton & Co., 1981.

Glickman, Simon. "Stokely Carmichael." In *Contemporary Black Biography*. Detroit: Gale Research, Inc., 1992.

Goldenberg, Boris. *The Cuban Revolution and Latin America*. New York: Frederick A. Praeger, Inc., 1966.

Granma (Havana), 16 January 1966–5 January 1969; and 8 October 1972.

Gray, Robert C., and Stanley J. Michalak, Jr. *American Foreign Policy since Détente*. New York: Harper & Row, 1984.

Guevara, Ernesto "Che." *The Complete Bolivian Diaries of Che Guevara*. Edited by Daniel James. London: George Allen & Unwim Ltd., 1968.

———. "Internationalism and Anti-Imperialism." *Tricontinental*, no. 2 (September–October 1967): 19–30.

———. "The Role We Must Play." *Tricontinental*, no. 2 (September–October 1967): 17–33.

———. *Socialism and Man in Cuba*. New York: Pathfinder Press, 1989.

———. "Tactics and Strategy of the Latin-American Revolution." *Tricontinental*, no. 2 (September–October 1967).

———. *Venceremos! The Speeches and Writings of Ernesto Che Guevara*. Edited by John Gerassi. New York: Simon and Schuster, 1968.

Hare, Nathan. "A Critique of Black Leaders." *The Black Scholar* (March–April 1972): 2–5.

Hilliard, David, and Lewis Cole. *This Side of Glory*. Boston: Little, Brown and Co., 1993.

Hodges, Donald C. *The Legacy of Che Guevara*. London: Thames and Hudson, Ltd., 1977.

Horowitz, Irving Louis. *American Foreign Policy toward Castro's Cuba: Paradox, Procrastination, and Paralysis*. Coral Gables, Fla.: University of Miami North-South Center, 1992.

———. *Cuban Communism*. New Brunswick, N.J.: Transaction, Inc., 1981.

Hutchinson, Earl Ofari. *Blacks and Reds: Race and Class in Conflict, 1919–1990.* East Lansing: Michigan State University Press, 1995.

Informe del Comité Central del Partido Comunista de Cuba sobre las activi-dades de la microfacción [Report of the Central Committee of the Cuban Communist Party on the Activies of the Micro-faction]. Havana: Instituto del Libro, 1968.

Johnson, Anne Janette. "Angela Davis." In *Contemporary Black Biography.* Detroit: Gale Research, Inc., 1992.

King, Martin Luther, Jr. *Stride Toward Freedom.* New York: Harper & Row, 1986.

Kornbluh, Peter, and James G. Blight. "Dialogue with Castro: A Hidden History." *The New York Review of Books* 41, no. 16 (6 October 1994): 1–4.

———, William D. Rogers, Philip Brenner, James Blight, and Wayne Smith. "The U.S. and Cuba: The Secret History of Efforts to Normalize Relations." Paper presented at the Latin American Studies Association (LASA) Conference, Washington, D.C., 29 September 1995.

Le Monde (Paris), 9 November 1963 and 30–31 January 1966.

Llovio-Menéndez, José Luis. *Insider: My Hidden Life as a Revolutionary in Cuba.* New York: Bantam Books, July 1988.

Löwy, Michael, ed. *Marxism in Latin America from 1909 to the Present.* Atlantic Highlands, N.J.: Humanities Press International, Inc., 1992.

"Malcolm X, Ho Chi Minh, José Martí." *Tricontinental Bulletin,* no. 30 (September 1968): 1.

Marable, Manning. *Through the Prism of Race and Class: Modern Black Nationalism in the U.S.–Working Papers in Progress.* Dept. of City and Regional Planning in Conjunction with the Program in Urban and Regional Studies, Cornell University, May 1980.

Marine, Gene. *The Black Panthers.* New York: The New American Library, Inc., 1969.

Marx, Karl, and Friedrich Engels. *The Communist Manifesto.* New York: Bantam Books, 1992.

Meier, August, John Bracey, Jr. and Elliott Rudwick. *Black Protest in the Sixties.* New York: Markus Wiener Publishing, Inc., 1991.

Mesa-Lago, Carmelo, ed. *Revolutionary Change in Cuba.* Pittsburgh: University of Pittsburgh Press, 1971.

Miller, James. *"Democracy is in the Streets:" From Port Huron to the Siege of Chicago*. New York: Simon and Schuster, 1987.

Ministerio de relaciones exteriores de Venezuela. "Seis años de agresión" [Six Years of Aggression]. Caracas: Ministerio de relaciones exteriores de Venezuela. Imprenta Nacional, 1966.

Moore, Dhoruba. "Strategies of Repression Against the Black Movement." *The Black Scholar* (May–June 1981): 10–16.

Murray, George, and Joudon Major Ford. "Black Panthers: The Afro-Americans' Challenge: Interview with George Murray and Joudon Major Ford." Havana: *Tricontinental*, no. 10 January–February 1969): 96–111.

The New York Times, 24 August 1969, 25 May 1973, 22 February 1998.

"The *New York Times*, Che Guevara, and the Cuban Revolution: A Further Exchange." *Militant* 59, no. 48 (14 December 1995): 7.

Newman, Philip C. "Results of Castro's Visit." *Foreign Policy Bulletin* 38, no. 17 (15 May 1959): 12–13.

Newton, Huey P. "Culture and Liberation." *Tricontinental*, no. 11 (March–April 1969): 101–4.

Newton, Huey P., and Bobby Seale. "The Black Panther." In *Black Nationalism in America*, ed. John H. Bracey, Jr., August Meier, and Elliott Rudwick. New York: The Bobbs-Merrill Company, Inc., 1970.

Newton, Michael. *Bitter Grain: Huey Newton and the Black Panther Party*. Los Angeles: Holloway House Publishing Company, 1991.

Newton, Michael, and Judy Ann Newton. *FBI Most Wanted, an Encyclopedia*. New York: Garland Publishing, Inc., 1989.

Ofari, Earl. "Marxism-Leninism—the Key to Black Liberation." *The Black Scholar* (September 1972): 35–46.

Oksenberg, Michel, and Robert B. Oxnam. *China and America Past and Future*. HEADLINE Series, no. 235. New York: The Foreign Policy Association, April 1977.

Pavlov, Yuri. *Soviet-Cuban Alliance: 1959–1991*. Coral Gables, Fla: University of Miami North-South Center, 1994.

Pérez, Louis A., Jr. *Cuba: Between Reform and Revolution*. New York: Oxford University Press, 1995.

Perkus, Cathy, ed. *COINTELPRO: The FBI's Secret War on Political Freedom*. New York: Monad Press, 1975.

Prado Salmón, Gary. *Como Capturé al Che* [How I Captured Che]. Barcelona, Spain: Ediciones B., 1987.

Ramparts magazine, ed. *Two, Three. . . Many Vietnams*. New York: Harper & Row, 1971.

"The Rebellion of the North American Black People." *Tricontinental Bulletin*, no. 30 (September 1968): 57–58.

Rodríguez, Carlos Rafaél. "Speech to the Conference of Communist and Workers Parties in Moscow." *Política Internacional* 7, no. 25, (1969).

Rojo, Ricardo. *My Friend Che*. New York: Grove Press, 1968.

Romero, Carlos Antonio. *Las Relaciones entre Venezuela y la URSS: Diplomacía o Revolución* [The Relations between Venezuela and the USSR: Diplomacy and Revolution]. Caracas: Universidad Central de Venezuela Consejo de Desarrollo Científico y Humanístico, 1992.

Rossi, Peter H., ed. *Ghetto Revolts*. New Brunswick, N.J.: Transaction Books, 1973.

Rubenstein, Richard E. *Rebels in Eden: Mass Political Violence in the United States*. Boston: Little, Brown and Company, 1970.

Sale, Kirkpatrick. *SDS*. New York: Random House, 1973.

Sauvage, Léo. *Che Guevara: The Failure of a Revolutionary*. Englewood Cliffs, N.J.: Prentice-Hall, Inc., 1973.

Semidei, Manuela. *Les Etats-Unis et la revolution cubaine* [The United States and the Cuban Revolution]. Paris: Presses de la Foundation Nationale des Sciences Politiques, 1968.

Shakur, Assata. *Assata: An Autobiography*. London: Zed Books, Ltd., 1987.

Sheehy, Gail. *Panthermania*. New York: Harper & Row, 1971.

Smith, Baxter. "FBI Memos Reveal Repression Schemes." *The Black Scholar* (April 1974): 43–48.

Smith, Tony. *Thinking Like a Communist*. New York: W.W. Norton & Company, 1987.

The Star Tribune, 13–14 July 1997.

Sobel, Lester A., ed. *Cuba, the U.S. and Russia, 1960–1963*. New York: Facts on File, 1964.

Spero, Sterling D., and Abram L. Harris. *The Black Worker*. New York: Columbia University Press, 1931.

Stanford, Max. "Black Guerilla Warfare: Strategy and Tactics." *The Black Scholar* (November 1970): 30–38.

Stoper, Emily. *The Student Nonviolent Coordinating Committee*. Brooklyn, N.Y.: Carlson Publishing Inc., 1989.

Suchlicki, Jaime. *University Students and Revolution in Cuba, 1920–1968.* Coral Gables, Fla.: University of Miami Press, 1969.

Tablada, Carlos. *Che Guevara: Economics and Politics in the Transition to Socialism.* New York: Pathfinder Press, 1990.

Thomas, Hugh. *Cuba, or the Pursuit of Freedom.* London: Eyre & Spottiswoode, 1971.

"To the Reader." *Tricontinental,* no. 2 (September–October 1967): np.

"United States: Armed Confrontation." *Tricontinental Bulletin,* no. 43 (October 1969).

"USA: from Little Rock to Urban Rebellions." *Tricontinental Bulletin,* no. 46 (January 1970): 6–16.

"Violence in the American Way of Life." *Tricontinental Bulletin,* 61 (April 1971): 24–30.

Walters, Ronald W. *Pan Africanism in the African Diaspora.* Detroit, Mich.: Wayne State University Press, 1993.

Watters, Pat. *Encounter with the Future.* Atlanta, Ga.: Southern Regional Council, 1965.

White, John. *Black Leadership in America.* New York: Longman Group, 1990.

Williams, Robert F. *Negroes with Guns.* New York: Marzani & Munsell, Inc., 1962.

X, Malcolm. *Malcolm X: In Our Own Image.* Edited by Joe Wood. New York: St. Martin's Press, 1992.

———. *Malcolm X Speaks. Selected Speeches and Statements.* Edited by George Breitman. New York: Pathfinder Press, 1989.

———. "USA: The Hour of Mau Mau." *Tricontinental,* no. 11 (March–April 1969): 30.

INDEX

Africa: Algeria, xv, 12, 33, 42; Angola, 117; Carmichael's exile in, xv, 59, 61, 129, 130; Cleaver's exile in, xv, 94, 119, 130; communism in, 32; Congo compared to other Black insurrection, xi; Congo conflicts in, xiii, 32, 42, 82, 117; Cuba supported by, 32; Cuba's focus on, 5, 32–33, 117, 102–21; decolonization, 32–33; guerrilla warfare in, 32–33; Guevara in, 28, 33, 42, 78; insurrection in 19, 32–33; Malcolm X in, xiii, 57–58. *See also* OSPAAAL
African American leaders. *See* Black leaders; Black-led revolution
African American struggles and the peace movement, 97–100
Afro-Asian Economic Seminar, 42
Afro-Asian Solidarity Conference, 45
Afro-Cuban population, 46–47, 81, 101,112, 113; Castro support by the, 46
Agrarian Reform Institute (INRA), 39
Algeria. *See* Africa
alliances: Black Movement and China, 28; Black Movement and Cuba, 19, 21–33; Cuba and the USSR, 19–20, 21, 25, 28; international contexts and, 19–33. *See also* Black Leaders; Black Movement; Castro, Fidel; Cuba; Guevara, Ernesto; USSR; U.S. Black-led revolution; U.S. government

Amuchastegui, Domingo, 17n. 2, 65, 66, 79, 88; Cleaver and, 93; on Cuban power imbalance, 113; on security, 92, 107
American Communist Party. *See* CPUSA
American Society of Newspaper Editors, 21
Anaya, Franklin, 6n. 5
Anderson, John Lee, 6n. 5
Angola, 117
Anthony, Earl, 118, 119
anti-imperialism. *See* Castro, Fidel
Anti-War Movement: Black Movement's role in, 78, 98–99, 127; CIA investigation of the, xvi; protests, xii. *See also* Vietnam
Arbenz, Jacobo, 42
Arbesu (liaison), 91, 94
Argentina, 30, 42, 120
Armed Deacons of Self-Defense (ADSD), 79
armed self-defense, xi, 11; Carmichael and, 62; communist reactions to, 77; Du Bois and, 55; King and, 52; Malcolm X and, 57. *See also* insurrection; Williams, Robert
Asia. *See* guerrilla warfare; Guevara, Ernesto; insurrection; OSPAAAL; Vietnam
asylum. *See* Cuba; exile
Atlanta, Georgia, xvi, 62

143